Contents

Positive Criminology

EDITORS
Michael R. Gottfredson
Travis Hirschi

SAGE PUBLICATIONS
The Publishers of Professional Social Science
Newbury Park Beverly Hills London New Delhi

For information address:

SAGE Publications, Inc.
2111 West Hillcrest Drive
Newbury Park, California 91320

SAGE Publications Inc.
275 South Beverly Drive
Beverly Hills
California 90212

SAGE Publications Ltd.
28 Banner Street
London EC1Y 8QE
England

SAGE PUBLICATIONS India Pvt. Ltd.
M-32 Market
Greater Kailash I
New Delhi 110 048 India

Printed in the United States of America

Library of Congress Cataloging-in-Publication Data

Main entry under title:

Positive criminology.

Bibliography: p.
1. Crime and criminals. 2. Positivism.
I. Gottfredson, Michael R. II. Hirschi, Travis.
HV6028.P67 1987 364 87-16447
ISBN 0-8039-2911-0

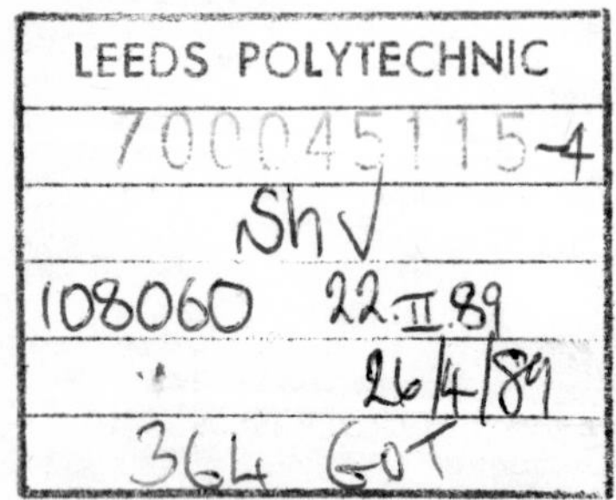

In Memoriam: Michael Hindelang

Michael Hindelang died in March 1982, at the age of 36. At the time of his death, he was Professor of Criminal Justice at the State University of New York at Albany, and President of the Criminal Justice Research Center. He had received bachelor's and master's degrees from Wayne State University in Detroit, his hometown, and a doctorate in criminology from the University of California at Berkeley in 1969. His first academic appointment was at California State University, Los Angeles, where he taught before joining the School of Criminal Justice at Albany in 1971.

In the ten years between his appointment at Albany and the onset of his illness, Michael Hindelang did as much as any scholar anywhere to bring the study of crime to academic respectability. He did so by insisting on establishing a factual base for the field, and by scrupulous adherence to the highest canons of scientific inquiry. In all of his work, from the creation of the *Sourcebook of Criminal Justice Statistics* (in 1973) to the many articles on such basic correlates of crime as age, sex, and race, Michael Hindelang demonstrated his devotion to criminology as an empirical science and his disdain for the ideological and political polemics that often characterized the field.

As a result of his efforts, the value for many purposes of criminological data from self-report, victimization, and even official sources is now generally acknowledged. It is no longer possible to dismiss the results of competent research simply by listing "potential" problems in the measures employed. And it is therefore no longer possible to claim that nothing is known about the causes and consequences of crime.

Michael Hindelang's impact on the field extends much beyond his extensive bibliography. His students occupy leading roles in many academic and research institutions in the country. All, we are sure, now think twice before regarding a piece of work as finished, and all, we are equally sure, recall with appreciation and affection the stern generosity of their mentor.

This book was assembled in his honor by friends of Michael Hindelang. Proceeds from its sale go to the Michael J. Hindelang Scholarship Fund administered by the Research Foundation of the

State University of New York. The editors solicited the chapters around a theme characteristic of Michael's work, a theme that quite naturally stimulates a variety of responses. No effort was made to impose a definition of positivism on the contributors. The introductory chapter by the editors was not meant to establish a theme for the book, but rather to show that the connection between classical criminology and positivism has been misunderstood. We hope this chapter, and those that follow it, can be taken to show that a major feature of positivism is a willingness to criticize its received point of view.

—Michael R. Gottfredson
—Travis Hirschi
Tucson, Arizona

1

The Positive Tradition

MICHAEL R. GOTTFREDSON
TRAVIS HIRSCHI

In the history section of their first survey course, criminology students learn the distinction between the positivists and the classicists. They learn that the positivists accepted the scientific idea that human behavior is determined, while the classicists believed in choice or freedom of the will. They also learn that, early in the twentieth century, the positivists, represented by Lombroso and Ferri, won the battle with the classicists, represented by Beccaria and Bentham, and thus elevated criminology to modern, scientific status.

After learning these important facts, the student hears little more about positivism or classicism until the course reaches the mid-1960s and "modern" theories of delinquency. At this point, the student is introduced to David Matza's *Delinquency and Drift* (1964), from which he or she learns that belief in determinism is old-fashioned, that criminology has not kept pace with current thinking in the philosophy of science, and that an alternative view of human behavior is easier to reconcile with the facts. This alternative view is, of course, the classical view, according to which the actor is free to choose one course of action rather than another.

Matza's work was only the beginning of the decline of positivism in criminology. His charge that criminologists were ignorant of modern trends in the philosophy of science was, by today's standards, mild criticism. According to more recent critics, positivism "dehumanizes man" (Phillipson, 1974: 3) and is synonymous with mindless acceptance of existing political arrangements (Quinney, 1975). It is probably true, as Greenberg (1981: 2) says, that "today the term 'positivist' is bandied about quite loosely, usually in a derogatory tone."

Greenberg's characterization of the view of most criminologists is probably correct. "Positivist" is usually derogatory. And it is also loosely used. We cannot easily change the view of the field that positivism is an inadequate or inappropriate approach to crime, but we can give some precision to the definition of the term. In our view, *positivism* represents the scientific approach to the study of crime where science is characterized by methods, techniques, or rules of procedure rather than by substantive theory or perspective. In other words, no theory of crime can claim a priori support from science or positivism.

Some of the looseness of the definition can be traced to failure to make this distinction between method and substance. Thus criminologists, especially perhaps sociological criminologists, are likely to conclude that acceptance of positivistic method requires positive theories of crime. They are also likely to conclude that acceptance of positivistic method carries with it ineluctable implications for criminal justice policy.

Positivism has thus had its fortunes reversed twice in criminology's history: first when it triumphed over the classical school and, second, when it was shown to be passé and primitive compared to the classical school. What is intriguing about these dramatic turns of fortune is that they seem to have sources external to the tenets of positivism itself. In both the triumph and the decline, positivism was argued to be an important source of the operating system of criminal justice. (It has been difficult for criminologists to resist drawing a connection between methods of learning and systems of action throughout their history.) Given this connection, the implications of failures in the system of action (the criminal justice system) seem obvious for the method of learning (positivism). Thus the tide of positivism in criminology has ebbed and flowed with the favor and disfavor of its putative theories and their putative policy implications.

In the period of triumph, the theory of crime implicit in the classical school was denounced in order to justify procedural changes in the justice system (e.g., excuses for crime based on age or mental illness). In the current period of decline, positivism is blamed for an unjust and discriminatory justice system that, among other things, fosters class justice (Greenberg, 1981) and the indeterminate sentence (Jeffery, 1972). It seems, however, that neither revolution has been particularly faithful to the tenets of positivism as practiced by ordinary criminologists. The history of positivistic criminology is thus badly in need of revision, and a good place to start is with the apparent victory of positivism over the classical school, where, historians argue, science defeated free will in the battle for the faith of criminologists.

POSITIVISM VERSUS THE CLASSICAL SCHOOL

The standard histories of criminology (Radzinowicz, 1963; Vold, 1958) tell of profound tension between the free will assumptions of classical theorists, most notably Beccaria, and the hard-nosed determinism of the positivists, such as Lombroso, Garofalo, and especially Ferri. Indeed, the literature in criminology continually reminds us of the conflict between the positive school and its assumption of determinism and even compulsion and the classical school and its assumption of free will and choice. Given compulsion on the one hand and choice on the other, the conflict between the two perspectives is indeed absolute, and is loaded with implications for theory and practice. One leads to concern for the causes of crime. The other focuses almost exclusively on deterrence.

Obviously, these distinctions between the deterministic assumptions of the positive school and the choice assumptions of the classical-deterrence school were overdrawn by those attempting to make criminology scientific. Consider, for example, Ferri's (1973: 244) attack on the methods he claimed underlay the classical school:

> For us, the experimental (i.e., inductive) method is the key to all knowledge; to them everything derives from logical deductions and traditional opinion. For them, facts should give place to syllogisms; for us the fact governs and no reasoning can occur without starting with facts. For them, science needs only paper, pen and ink and the rest comes from a brain stuffed with more or less abundant reading of books made with the same ingredients. For us, science requires spending a long time in examining facts one by one, evaluating them, reducing them to a common denominator, extracting the central idea from them. For them a syllogism or an anecdote suffices to demolish a myriad of facts gathered through years of observation and analysis; for us the reverse is true.

If the methods by which the classical school made claims to knowledge were so obviously defective, then the theory of crime implicit in their perspective (that crime is caused by the absence of restraints) must also be defective. But Ferri and the other early positivists were less interested in the crime causation aspects of classical thought than in reform of the criminal justice system. Again, consider Ferri (1968: 37-38):

> Among the fundamental bases of criminal and penal law as heretofore understood are these three postulates:
>
> (1) The criminal has the same ideas, the same sentiments as any other man.
>
> (2) The principal effect of punishment is to arrest the excess and the increase of crime.
>
> (3) Man is endowed with free will or moral liberty; and for that reason, is morally guilty and legally responsible for his crimes.
>
> On the other hand, one has only to go out of the scholastic circle of juridical studies and "a priori" affirmations, to find in opposition to the preceding assertions, these conclusions of the experimental sciences:
>
> (1) Anthropology shows by facts that the delinquent is not a normal man; that on the contrary he represents a special class, a variation of the human race through organic and physical abnormalities, either hereditary or acquired.
>
> (2) Statistics prove that the appearance, increase, decrease, or disappearance of crime depends upon other reasons than the punishments prescribed by the codes and applied by the courts.
>
> (3) Positive psychology has demonstrated that the pretended free will is a purely subjective illusion.

By throwing out the assumption of a free will as a basis for a legal code, the early positivists threw out, they hoped, the criminal justice system spawned by classical logic. They also threw out, at the same time, the theory of crime causation implicit in classical thought. Ironically, then, the scientific method excluded a theory of crime and a system of criminal justice on clearly nonscientific grounds, on the idea that science makes substantive claims about human nature and society, rather than on the principle of empirical falsification or (in the case of the criminal justice system) scientific evaluation. This error was and is made because criminologists, from Ferri to the present, overdraw the assumption of determinism.

As a central working assumption, determinism implies that all behavior is the product of antecedent causes. The task is to associate variability in causal factors with variability in crime until all crime has been explained. No deterministic explanation of crime can reasonably exclude the variables of the classical model on deterministic grounds. These variables may account for some of the variation in crime. If so, they have as much claim to inclusion in a "positivistic" model as any other set of variables accounting for the same amount of variation.

The illusion of conflict between determinism and free will has been further perpetuated by an overly narrow notion of general deterrence. As the term has come to be applied in the literature, *general deterrence* is the reduction in crime in the population as a whole that results from imposition of legal sanctions on persons convicted of crime. Typically, this definition does not arise from a clear perspective on crime causation, but from a research tradition tied to a narrow set of available indicators of crime rates and sanction levels.

It is an unfortunate artifact of the historical development of classical criminology that the idea of general deterrence came to be associated solely with legal penalties and to be divorced from the more powerful sanctions that may attend rule violations, such as those available to families and communities. But as mentioned, the classicists were interested primarily in a theory that would implicate and constrain the state, and they were therefore interested primarily in the impact of the criminal law. Such policy purposes are clearly not integral to the deterrence notion. The idea at the heart of the notion of general deterrence is that people fail to commit crime out of fear. The opponents of the logic of deterrence suggest there is only one source of fear worth mentioning, legal punishment. But most of us fail to violate the law much of the time because we fear losing the respect of those we care about (see Kornhauser, 1978).

To say that people do not commit criminal acts because they are afraid of what others may think of them if they do, or because they may see such acts as impeding their progress toward some cherished goal, is not to deny the preventive effects of legal restraints. Both social and legal restraints are legitimate aspects of the idea of general deterrence. But the point is that both allow "free will" in the sense that the individual may choose to ignore the wishes of his or her parents, to forget the cherished goal, or to ignore the legal consequences of the act and proceed to commit it. In which case, it seems reasonable to suspect that the hedonic calculus of Benthan and Beccaria may be at work. At the same time, it is equally correct to argue that (to the extent the theory is true) crime is caused by a lack of restraint, that it is therefore determined. If the threat of legal action did not exist, it could not cause someone to fail to commit an offense. Similarly, if there were no love to be lost, there could be no fear of losing it. General deterrence may simply be more general than most criminologists give it credit for being.

Members of the classical school would not deny this extension of the idea of deterrence. They were interested in legal punishment and responsibility, and their theories were theories of the administration of justice. Beccaria's purpose was to define and limit the scope of criminal sanctions. For him, deterrence theory set natural and reasonable limits on state punishments. His principal focus was on legal punishments as a defense of human freedoms. "Free will" was thus a necessary component in the social contract because it established that society exists at the request of the people *to protect their rights.* Free will implied responsibility, choice, and rationality as elements of the social contract. But there was nowhere the idea that the will of the people could not be influenced, shaped, or changed. Nor did Becarria imply that legal penalties are the only source of the fear that prevents criminal acts or even the most important source of the fear that might influence the will. The focus on legal restraints flowed from the purposes of the classical theorist, to achieve a moderate legal system with rules of procedure. Nothing in the classical theory suggests that there are no individual or group differences in the susceptibility of the will to influence. In short, the classical school is in principle, if not in common construction, compatible with the idea of determinism. As such, it has the same logical foundation as the "positive theories."

Nevertheless, in the first confrontation between positivism and the classical school, the victory of the positivists was decisive. Deterrence, in all its manifestations, was relegated to the realm of the unscientific, and free will became just another ancient superstition, along with magic, witchcraft, and the devil. Modern scholars were thus able to forge convincing links among a particular brand of theorizing (naturally good people are impelled to crime by individual or social circumstance), policy choices, and the scientific method. If the method was accepted, as it must be accepted, then the theory and the policy came with it. This was not to be the last time an intellectual victory was won by forging a link between the method of science and the substance of a particular theory. The recent decline of positivism may be traced to the same logical process.

THE FALL FROM GRACE

In 1964, when David Matza published his influential critique of theories of delinquency causation, *Delinquency and Drift*, the prospects for scientific criminology seemed better than they had ever seemed before. Powerful theoretical statements had begun to emerge, each tied to respected master theories of the social and behavioral sciences. Some of these theories asserted the hegemony of an established school over the raw material of delinquent behavior (Redl and Wineman, 1951; Miller, 1958). Others applied popular social theories to the facts of delinquency, yielding explanations that seemed to fit these facts and to be more generally "correct" (Cloward and Ohlin, 1960). Still others reflected deeply about the nature of theory, and about the complementary relations among disciplines, producing elegant statements honed to the realities of modern society (Cohen, 1955).

Indeed, the power of these theories seemed to obviate the need for the theorist to examine in detail the findings of research. All that was needed was a general *portrait* of the delinquent, a portrait that could be painted along with (deduced from?) the statement of the theory. As long as the theorist did not stray too far from what the man on the street could tell him about delinquency (i.e., that groups of young lower-class boys do most of it), everything else could be pretty much (and better) left alone. The theorist could assume, without too much trouble from colleagues in the social sciences, that everything one needed to know about delinquency was already known.

It looked as though the science of criminology had evolved from the chaos of the positivistic multiple-factor approach of the 1940s and 1950s to all-encompassing theories capable of explaining the meaning of just about everything. At last, criminology could be concerned with theoretical issues rather than narrow and often apparently pointless fact gathering. And with this thought in mind, research testing the new theories began in earnest, using the most sophisticated tools of the social sciences (Short and Strodtbeck, 1965).

Although no one since Enrico Ferri (1973) had spent much time defining and defending the positivistic approach, modern American criminologists, such as Glueck and Glueck (1950) and Shaw and McKay (1929), acted as though they knew how positivists were supposed to behave: One operationally defined the subject matter, gathered evidence relative to it, and then made public the definition, the method of gathering evidence, and the evidence itself. But if things looked smooth on the surface, strong crosscurrents lurked below. Many criminologists were simply uncomfortable with the plethora of "facts" generated by positivistic research. Although not denying the existence or possibility of correlates of crime, these theorists were most comfortable when such facts were subordinate to theory. Indeed, the idea that facts are nothing more than the preconceptions of researchers was about to be stated in articulate form. In order to free criminology and its theories from positivistic competition, a metaphysic that demeaned data had to be invented.

Given the dominance of sociology in criminology and the strength within sociology of interactionist and conflict theories, it was not difficult for criminologists to adopt an antipositivistic metaphysic. Although the sources of this metaphysic may be disputed, one current statement will suffice to demonstrate that it has arrived:

> [*Positivism*] generally refers to criminology characterized by one or more of the following assumptions: (1) The causes of crime are deterministic . . . and pathological. (2) Criminal behavior can be explained without reference to the meaning that the behavior has for the criminal actor. (3) Crime and criminals exist as phenomena independently of whether the behavior and persons in question are regarded as criminal by the government or the public at large. (4) Crime can be studied through the same methods (quantitative statistical techniques) and with the same goals (the formulation of historically invariant laws) as the natural sciences. (5) The government can and should take steps to eliminate the causes of crime, drawing on scientific knowledge provided by criminologists [Greenberg, 1981: 2].

Apart from the assumption of determinism, none of the other "assumptions" listed has an ineluctable connection to positivism. This strategy is, however, common. Positivism is described as a set of substantive or theoretical assumptions that no self-respecting modern social scientist could accept. In addition to the cleansing effect this provides critics, it also allows them frankly to admit their own biases and assumptions that will thereafter be regarded as off-limits to empirical test. The advantage of having a "theory" that is beyond the reach of empirical test is obviously enormous.

While Greenberg's "assumptions of positivism" are an odd lot, they serve to illustrate the ease with which critics of positivism move between logical and political criticism of the positivistic approach. If positivism requires pathological causes, mindless criminals, and governmental intervention, something evil cannot be far away. Indeed, modern critics of positivism delight in suggesting that scientific criminology is totalitarian in essence. For example, George Vold (1958: 35-36), who defines positivism as "the application of a deterministic and scientific method to the study of crime," also says:

> [One] of the implications of positivistic theory . . . [is] the ease with which it fits into totalitarian patterns of government. . . . There is an obvious

> similarity in conception of the control of power in society between positivism and the political reality of centralized control of the life of the citizen by a government bureaucracy indifferent to democratic public opinion.

Vold's evidence for linking positivism with a preference for totalitarianism was that Ferri, a former Marxist, became a member of Italy's fascist party in his declining years (subsequent to his major works from a positivistic perspective). Still, when forced to choose between science and democracy, it is not surprising that modern criminologists have chosen the latter, uncritically accepting Vold's leap of logic. Looking into a positivistic future and not liking what they have seen, these criminologists have decided in advance that research based on the idea that individual differences cause crime will invariably have insidious implications for the criminal justice system. Absent in the work of these concerned criminologists, however, is a logical or factual demonstration that specific policies are suggested by causal knowledge, a point that would a priori seem important for them to attempt to make.

If Vold's logic is defective, it is not unusual. Many scholars link positivism to specific criminal justice practices and programs. Take, for example, C. Ray Jeffery's (1972: 488) definition of positivism:

> The basic postulates of positivistic criminology are (1) a rejection of legal concepts of crime and criminal procedure, and their replacement with individualized justice based on a therapeutic mode, (2) a rejection of punishment and its replacement with correctional treatment, (3) a rejection of free will and its replacement with scientific determinism, and (4) a rejection of the study of criminal law, and its replacement with a study of the individual offender and his medical, psychological, and social characteristics.

Again, we see the link being forged among the assumptions of the scientific method and particular criminal justice policies (and even, in Vold and Greenberg, preferences about the form of government). Thus if a criminologist believes that (a) there are differences in behavior, (b) that there are differences in individual and social circumstance that produce these differences in behavior, and (c) that both sets of differences and their correspondence can be observed and measured by public rules, then this criminologist must, according to Greenberg, Vold, and Jeffery, (a) oppose punishment for criminal offenders, (b) oppose rules of criminal procedure, (c) have no natural curiosity about the causes of human behavior, (d) have no interest in the study of criminal law, and (e) be a lackey for the oppressive forces of government.

This list is not only fatuous, it is internally inconsistent as well. But the point of such critiques of positivism is not to display crisp logic; it is to undermine a method of knowing so obviously defective that it cannot be slandered. And the scientist who believes that

(a) some children choose to disobey their parents by committing crimes, because
(b) their parents are unwilling or unable to do anything about their disobedience, and
(c) that such children should be punished by the juvenile justice system, but
(d) only subsequent to a fair ajudication premised on procedural rules,

cannot exist—regardless of the evidence that such people do exist.

TODAY'S POSITIVISM

In light of the pervasive distaste for positivism expressed by many modern criminologists, it is surprising to discover that positivistic criminology may today be healthier than ever. What are the sources or strengths of positivism that have allowed it to thrive under such unrelenting attack? For one thing, positivism has given up a claim to isomorphism with particular substantive theories of crime and particular criminal justice policies. As a result, the failure of a theory is no longer evidence that the method is defective, and the failure of a program is no longer cause to reexamine the connection between criminology and science. As another result, positivists now feel no need to obliterate the choice theories so passionately criticized by positivism's founders. In fact, such theories are now increasingly regarded as legitimately within the scientific domain (witness the report by a panel of the National Academy of Sciences, which not only investigated aspects of deterrence but concluded that the evidence leans in its favor). The only theories now considered archaic by positivists are the single-discipline, monolithic theories of an age gone by, theories such as the constitutional theories of biology and differential association of sociology.

Other trends that give modern positivism strength are well represented by the chapters to follow. In the aggregate, these trends reveal what is perhaps a healthier and more self-assured positivistic criminology than has heretofore existed.

The Unification of Empirical and Theoretical Criminology

Prior to about 1950, American positive criminology was heavily empirical. The principal research scholars (e.g., Sheldon Glueck and

Eleanor Glueck, Clifford Shaw and Henry McKay) were struggling to uncover the major patterns in crime and delinquency. The causal ideas in their studies were important antecedents of current theories, but their essential contribution was a set of hard-won, reliable facts necessary to a scientific criminology.

If the first half of the twentieth century was a period of empiricism, the next twenty years constituted a period of theorizing. The most influential books of the 1950s and 1960s, Cohen's *Delinquent Boys*, Cloward and Ohlin's *Delinquency and Opportunity*, and Matza's *Delinquency and Drift*, were as different from the empirical research of the earlier period as night from day. These were all theories produced from the top down, derived directly from major sociological perspectives.

This disjunction between research on the one hand and theory on the other is no longer part of the positivist tradition. Examples in the subsequent chapters are numerous, but include the chapters by Lawrence Cohen and Kenneth Land and by James Garofalo. Each of these authors has collected and analyzed a good amount of data. Each, too, has contributed to criminological theory. The chapter by Cohen and Land represents an extension of the routine activity theory developed by them and Marcus Felson, and an effort to link this perspective with control theory. Similarly, the chapter by Garofalo elaborates on his data-based theory of the causes of victimization, and emphasizes the current trend to make researchers and theorists the same person. Both chapters, incidentally, demonstrate that it is unsatisfactory for theoretical criminology to divide the field of crime causation into victim and offender studies. The striking feature of offending and victimization studies is the identity of their empirical correlates. This suggests a common explanation. Both the Cohen and Land and the Garofalo chapters, with their stress on opportunities for crime and the suitability of targets for offenses, add an important dimension to modern positivistic crime causation theories.

A Respect for Data

Certainly one feature of positive criminology has always been its belief in an objective external reality capable of measurement. Public disclosure of the understood reality, the procedures used for its measurement, and frequent independent replication are essential tenets of this perspective. But there has always been considerable skepticism about the quality of criminological data and considerable fear of being misled by measurement error. Fortunately, as John Laub's chapter demonstrates, significant advances have been made recently in our knowledge of the properties of measurement and how these properties affect the portrait of crime painted by major data bases. The result is that positivistic criminology is in better shape than ever with respect to confidence in the correlates of crime revealed in the data. Those theories spawned by fear of measurement error and the belief that the structure in crime data was produced by measurement bias, such as labeling theory, are now rejected by positivists.

To say that increased confidence in the data is a modern trend in positive criminology is not to suggest a lack of critical attention to measurement issues. On the contrary, today's empirical criminologists are, in measurement terms, able to appreciate true variance despite the presence of some error. That such a stance is *novel* would certainly shock most scientists, and stands as one mark of the depths to which positive criminology sank in the not too distant past.

A Renewed Emphasis on Basic Correlates

Coincident with a renewed faith in the veracity of criminological data is a renewed emphasis on the correlates of crime. The chapters by Joseph Weis on social class, by Robert Sampson on communities, and by Rodney Stark, Lori Kent, and Roger Finke on sports are examples of this trend in modern positivism.

Such emphasis is part and parcel of the trend toward empirically attentive theory and renewed faith in the data. Recent work in this tradition searches simultaneously for the nature of the principal crime correlates (i.e., magnitude and conditions of existence) and their interpretation. No longer are positivists content to examine anything and everything in relation to crime, to construct a scoreboard of pluses and minuses, and then move on to another nominated correlate. Today, as these chapters suggest, the empirical pattern and its meaning tend to receive equal attention.

The significance of this approach is great. It means, for example, that theories must be explicit about the correlates they predict, must indeed make predictions, and are of value only when they give meaning to the agreed upon correlates of crime. Furthermore, this trend suggests that nothing is off limits, that no piece of conventional wisdom is beyond investigation. Although a healthy skepticism has long been part of the positivist tradition, today it is no longer possible for fashionable theories to suppress research evidence contrary to them. This point could not be better made than by Weis's chapter, which begins with a premise contrary to most sociological theory, the premise that social class is an important correlate of crime.

Theory and Research Are Eclectic and Multidisciplinary

Modern positivism is impatient with disciplinary boundaries. The division of labor within universities that puts criminology in departments of sociology has, to some extent, been superseded by the creation of schools and departments of criminology and criminal justice. Psychologists, economists, and biologists with interest in crime and justice are finding a home in these departments and an interest on the part of journals in their work. Although sociology's domination of the discipline is not extinguished, the day is gone when the field would denigrate interdisciplinary work.

The chapters by Hans Toch and John Goldkamp represent this trend. Toch, a psychologist, is at home discussing the results of competent research, no matter the disciplinary source. To him, the test is advancement of knowledge, not the label after the scholar's name. Toch's chapter is convincing evidence that our theories of crime causation and our methods must be eclectic. There is no single method whereby positivistic knowledge is advanced. Toch argues for an incorporation of methods and perspectives many believe to be outside the scope of positivism.

Goldkamp's chapter contrasts nicely with Toch's. Goldkamp discusses the assumptions of modern behavioral psychology and points out the similarity between these assumptions and those of the early positivists.

Freedom to Take or Leave Policy Studies

Positive criminology may have been born out of concern for the justice system implications of causal theories, but the current trend is to acknowledge that the relation between causal theory and policy prescription is not straightforward. To understand the causes of crime does not imply that a solution is at hand. There is first the fact that once a cause has done its work, crime may be little affected by remediation of the cause. But it may also be true that remediation itself may tread too hard on political, social, or moral values, the preservation of which is thought to be more important than the potential benefits of crime reduction. (To the scientist, of course, such concerns are constraints operating in the world of action, not impediments to objective inquiry.)

The modern positivist feels comfortable working in both "applied" and "basic" settings, in large part because the methods of proof are now largely agreed to be similar. Despite the advent of the academic specialty of "evaluation studies," both applied and basic criminology look to the true, randomized experiment as the standard for inference. A common preference for rigorous methodology, including public measurement and replication, is the tie that binds academic and applied researchers together.

At the same time, modern positivism does not seem to *require* application of its theories or relevance to basic theory from its evaluation studies. In this respect, criminology may be paving the way for less self-confident subfields of the social and behavioral sciences.

Few scholars are as qualified to speak to such questions as Leslie Wilkins. His contributions to design and to applied criminology are substantial, ranging from the early studies of the effectiveness of treatments to the development and implementation of parole and sentence guidelines. Wilkins's chapter on policy continues his inquiry into the complex interplay between science and public policy.

CONCLUSION

By definition, positivists are optimists. As these chapters illustrate, such optimism is well-founded. The knowledge base of criminology is now broader and more secure than ever before. Major advances have been made in theory and in measurement techniques. Criminologists are now interdisciplinary and eclectic in ways only imagined earlier. Clearly, scientific criminology has survived a lean period and is now ready, once again, to flourish.

2

Reassessing the Lifestyle Model of Criminal Victimization

JAMES GAROFALO

Most adherents of positive criminology are actively engaged in empirical research. The primary motivation driving most researchers is probably the joy derived from doing research—a sort of "detective motive." However, unlike Chandler's Marlow or Hammet's Continental Op, the researcher does not arrive at a final answer to a self-contained problem at the end of each detection effort; the "case" is never "solved" because the "case" is always just one aspect of the complex, interconnected, changing web of social reality.

This lack of finality in the empirical research on which positive criminology is based could generate pessimism were it not for another aspect of positive criminology that is a theme of this book—namely, the belief that knowledge is cumulative. We will never find final answers, but each increment of knowledge enhances our abilities to understand and deal with our world.

Of course, the findings from diverse research efforts are most enlightening and most likely to contribute to a culmination of knowledge when they can be linked together in systematic frameworks—in theories or models. The stance of positive criminology is that theories and models should be used rather than enshrined. Theories and models should not become segregated from research; they should derive from, generate, and respond to research.

The guiding orientation of this chapter is that theories and models should not be static. They should be reassessed continually in the light of (a) research on the hypotheses they generate, and (b) criticisms of their concepts and logical structures. The subject of the chapter is the lifestyle model of criminal victimization that Michael Hindelang, Michael Gottfredson, and I developed between 1975 and 1977, and published in 1978. The model was grounded in the findings of our research with victimization survey data, and it has generated additional research and discussion in the years since it was published. My purpose here is to take the next step: to examine the model in the light of subsequent research and discussion, and to make any modifications that might be necessary to improve the model.

The book in which the model was presented (*Victims of Personal Crime: An Empirical Foundation for a Theory of Personal Victimization*) used victimization survey data from a number of U.S. cities to explore a variety of issues: the nature of injury and property loss in personal victimizations; the characteristics of nonvictims, victims, and people victimized repeatedly; fear of crime and perceptions of the crime problem. Despite the diversity of topics covered in the book, the attention of most readers apparently focused on the chapter in which we tried to pull findings together and develop a model—based on the concept of lifestyle—that would account for variations in the likelihood of becoming the victim of a personal crime.

This chapter begins with a recapitulation of the lifestyle model and a similar model, the routine activity approach (Cohen and Felson, 1979a), which was developed at about the same time. Pertinent criticisms of the lifestyle model are then raised and answered. This is followed by a discussion of relevant research reported since the model was developed. Finally, a revised lifestyle model is suggested, and policy implications of the model are discussed.

OVERVIEWS OF THE LIFESTYLE AND ROUTINE ACTIVITY MODELS

Figure 2.1 presents the lifestyle model as it first appeared in *Victims of Personal Crime* (Hindelang et al., 1978: 243). Basically, *lifestyle*—which we defined as routine daily activities, both vocational (work, school, keeping house, and so on) and leisure activities—is depicted as determining the likelihood of personal victimization through the intervening variables of associations and exposure. Moving from right to left, back through the model, lifestyle patterns are determined by individual and group adaptations to structural constraints and role

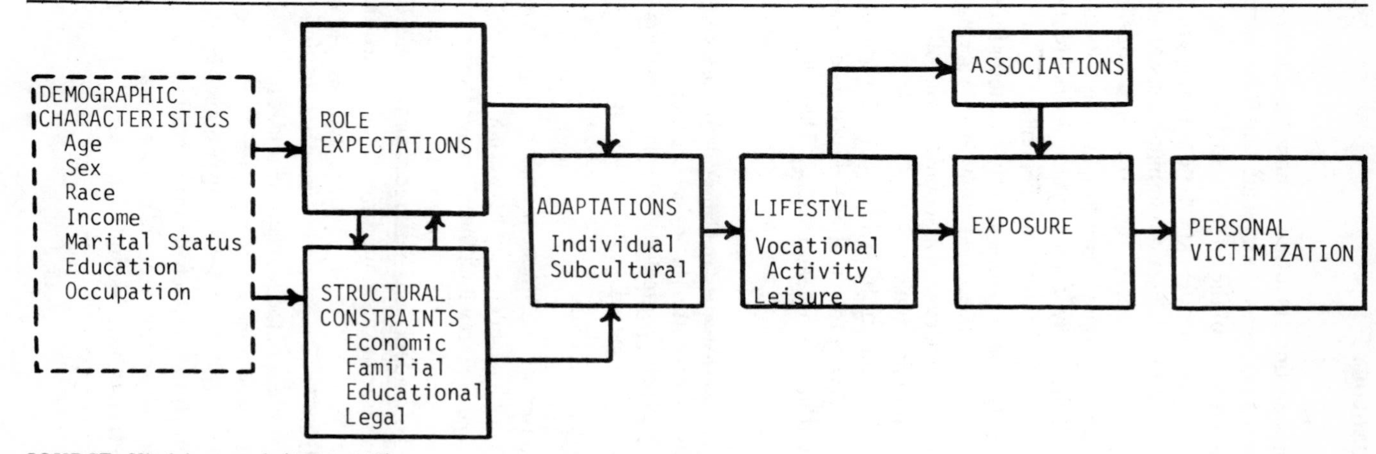

SOURCE: Hindelang et al. (1978: 243).

Figure 2.1 Original Lifestyle Model of Personal Victimization

expectations. The broken line enclosing demographic characteristics (age, sex, race, and so on) is meant to indicate that these variables are not part of the causal sequence of the model; rather, they are indicators of the structural constraints and role expectations that shape lifestyle.

The model is grounded in analyses of victimization data and other sources of information about crime. Victimization is not distributed randomly across space and time—there are high-risk locations and high-risk time periods. Similarly, some characteristics are disproportionately represented among criminal offenders relative to the general population—there are high-risk persons. Lifestyle patterns influence (a) the amount of exposure to places and times with varying risks of victimization, and (b) the prevalence of associations with others who are more or less likely to commit crimes.

At about the same time that the lifestyle model was being developed, Cohen and Felson (1979a) were formulating a similar model, which they referred to as a "routine activity approach." They defined *routine activities* as

> any recurrent and prevalent activities which provide for basic population and individual needs, whatever their biological or cultural origins. Thus routine activities would include formalized work, as well as the provision of standard food, shelter, sexual outlet, leisure, social interaction, learning and child rearing [Cohen and Felson, 1979a: 593].

Cohen and Felson focused on "direct-contact predatory violations": those "involving direct physical contact between at least one offender and at least one person or object which that offender attempts to take or damage" (p. 589). In order for these offenses to occur, three minimal elements—motivated offenders, suitable targets, and absence of capable guardians—must converge in space and time. They argued that, in the United States since World War II, routine activities have shifted increasingly away from the home and toward interactions between people who are not members of the same household. These changes have resulted in greater exposure of people to potential offenders outside the home and, concomitantly, in less time spent at home. In terms of the minimal elements for direct-contact predatory violations, more time spent away from home with nonhousehold members makes people more suitable targets for face-to-face victimization, while greater absence from the home decreases the presence of guardians of household property, making households more suitable targets.

There are a number of similarities between the lifestyle model and the routine activity approach. For example, neither tries to explain the motivation of offenders; criminal inclination is taken as a given, and attention is shifted to the contexts that allow the inclinations to be translated into action (see Cohen and Felson, 1979a: 589). In addition, both deal with patterned behavior among population aggregates rather than with variability in individual characteristics (such as the psychological propensity to "precipitate" violent interaction); thus the lifestyle model and the routine activity approach are sociological in their orientation.

The apparent differences between the lifestyle and routine activity models relate to how they were explicated by their authors rather than to differences in substance. For example, Cohen and Felson used the routine activity approach to link changes in the patterns of behavior of the aggregate U.S. population to changes in crime rates, and they examined a range of crimes that included direct thefts of property in which the victim was not present. In contrast, Hindelang, Gottfredson, and Garofalo related differences in lifestyles of population segments at one point in time to differences in victimization rates, and focused their attention more narrowly on crimes that involved direct contact between the victim and offender (personal crimes). However, it is implicit that both the lifestyle model and the routine activity approach are applicable cross-sectionally and longitudinally, and as was pointed out in its original presentation (Hindelang et al., 1978: 272). The lifestyle model is also relevant to other types of crimes, particularly household burglary, noncommercial larceny, and vehicle theft.

The discussion that follows, then, can be made to apply to either the lifestyle model or the routine activity approach. However, the discussion will be specific to the lifestyle model because of my involvement in that model's development.

CRITICISMS

There are three major criticisms directed at theories that use lifestyle, or a related mechanism, to explain victimization. Actually, the first two are best described as dangers to be avoided rather than as criticisms. These two will be addressed in the present section. The third criticism will be mentioned at the end of this section, but will be dealt with later in the chapter.

First, the lifestyle concept can be used in a way that makes the theory true by definition, and, therefore, uninformative and trivial. This occurs if the theory is reduced to a form that says, in effect: People who are not themselves exposed—or whose property is not exposed—to potential offenders have no risk of victimization. But lifestyle-type theories are really not reducible to this form. A convenient way of approaching the issue is to draw on the differentiation, recently made by Gottfredson (1981), between absolute and probabilistic exposure to risk. Absolute exposure is a necessary condition for victimization to occur: The victim (a person or property) must come into contact with the offender for the crime to occur. But victimization is not assured whenever simple contact takes place. Offenders do not commit crimes in every instance in which they come into contact with potential victims; other aspects of the situation must be conducive to offending (e.g., the offender must believe that he or she can complete the crime successfully). Thus the more frequently a person (or piece of property) is exposed to potential offenders in situations that are highly conducive to the commission of a crime, the higher the likelihood that the person (or property) will become the object of victimization—that is probabilistic exposure.

Another approach to this criticism is to think of lifestyle as determining levels of risk that exceed or fall below the average risk in society (see Smith, 1982). This approach even suggests a way to link the routine activity concept with the lifestyle model. As presented by Cohen and Felson, the aggregate structure of routine activities in a society affects the aggregate rate of victimization in the society. The structure of routine activities is subject to change over time, and these changes can be helpful in explaining changes in rates of victimization. However, at any given point in time, the structure of routine activities can be viewed as influencing the average likelihood of victimization in a society. Since the lifestyle model focuses on differences among subgroups of a society, it can be seen as attempting to account for deviations from the average likelihood of victimization in a society.

The second criticism of the lifestyle model pertains to how the model is used. The criticism is that the model creates a strong temptation for *ex post facto* explanations. Given the vagueness of the lifestyle concept, it is easy to account for correlations, or their absence, between victimization and various factors by claiming that some of the factors (those showing an association) are indicators of lifestyle, while others are not. This, however, makes the theory virtually nonfalsifiable.

The ideal way to handle this criticism is readily apparent: Simply develop a rigorous definition of lifestyle and specify the variables that are indicators of the concept in advance. In practice, the ideal is difficult to fulfill. There is no widespread agreement on a definition of lifestyle and on the variables that are indicators of lifestyle (see Sobel, 1981). Equally important is the fact that researchers seeking to analyze the lifestyle-victimization relationship generally do not have the luxury of specifying the indicators they want and developing data collection instruments that will generate the exact indicators desired. More often, researchers are faced with the necessity of conducting secondary analyses of data collected for other purposes, and, therefore, using whatever indicators happen to be present in the data. I have yet to see a victimization study designed primarily to test lifestyle-type models (although the items included in the recent British Crime Survey indicate a movement toward using victimization surveys for theory testing). Perhaps the reason is that victimization studies are relatively expensive, and there appears to be a belief that research into the lifestyle-victimization link will not produce insights that are directly applicable to public policy development. The issue of policy relevance is the basis for the third criticism of the lifestyle model, and I will defer addressing that issue until later in the chapter. The next section reviews relevant research findings that have accumulated since the lifestyle and routine activity models were presented.

RECENT RESEARCH FINDINGS

Continuation of Cohen's Work

Cohen and his colleagues have used the National Crime Survey victimization data to examine models of the lifestyle/routine activity type from a variety of perspectives. Their findings for personal larceny of two types (Cohen and Cantor, 1980), personal robbery (Cohen et al., 1981b), and residential burglary (Cohen and Cantor, 1981) generally support the predictions from the model. There were, however, some differences in the relationships found for the different types of crimes.

In the multivariate analysis of robbery—the type of direct-contact victimization on which the development of the lifestyle model was based—Cohen et al. (1981b) found that age, race, income, household size (a dichotomy of living alone versus not living alone), and major activity (a trichotomy of employed, unemployed, and home centered) were all related to the likelihood of victimization in the predicted direction. Specifically, blacks, the young, and people with low incomes (who are more likely to interact with potential robbery offenders) had higher risks than whites, older persons, and those with higher incomes; persons living alone (who, by definition, spend less time in the company of household members) had higher risks than persons not living alone; and the risk of robbery was highest for the unemployed, about average for the employed, and less than average for the home centered (assumedly reflecting different levels of exposure outside the home). When the joint effects of these factors were considered, the differences in robbery risk were striking. For example, the risk was 9.85 times higher than the national average among young (16-29), unemployed, low-income blacks who lived alone, but it was only 0.13 of the national average among older (50+), home-centered, high-income whites who did not live alone. Note that sex was not even considered in this analysis because there were too few female robbery victims in the sample.

When Cohen and Cantor (1981) examined residential burglary, the associations with risk were again evident for age and race (of the head of the household). Because the nature of the target in burglary is different than the target in personal crimes, Cohen and Cantor used different indicators of exposure and guardianship. As an indicator of propinquity to potential burglars, they determined whether the household was located in the central city of a SMSA, outside the central city of a SMSA, or completely outside of a SMSA. They also used an indicator of the amount of time that households were occupied, dichotomizing the sample into those households in which there was "at least one household member who did not go to school or engage in work at least fifteen hours per week" and those not having at least one such member (Cohen and Cantor, 1981: 118). As predicted, the risk of burglary was greatest for households located in central cities and designated as "less occupied."

But the variation of risk across income categories showed a different pattern for residential burglary than it did for robbery. The risk of burglary was highest in the bottom-income category, but next highest in the top-income category; middle-income households had the lowest risk of burglary. Cohen and Cantor explain this pattern by noting that income is really an indicator of two factors: the location of a household vis-à-vis areas with high concentrations of offenders, and the attractiveness of the household target. Low-income households are more likely to be in close proximity to potential offenders, while high-income households represent more attractive targets.

In their analysis of personal larceny, Cohen and Cantor (1980) reported results parallel to those from their robbery analysis for several variables: Risks were higher for the young, persons living alone, and persons whose major activity was housekeeping. However, blacks and whites had roughly similar risks when the other variables were taken into account, and the main effect of income showed increasing risk with increasing income. When one considers the nature of the larcenies examined by Cohen and Cantor, the race and income findings are not too puzzling. Like most of the robberies they studied, all of the personal larcenies occurred outside the home, and this could lead one to predict a higher risk for blacks and low-income persons because of their greater exposure to potential offenders. But, unlike robberies, almost all of the personal larcenies involved no contact between the victim and offender; they were primarily thefts of visible, unattended property, such as the theft of a camera from a parked car, a coat from a restaurant, luggage from an airport, and so forth. Given the nature of personal larceny, it is not surprising that people who are more likely to possess the kinds of goods that make attractive targets have higher risks of being victimized.

Studies Using Direct Indicators of Lifestyle

Corrado et al. (1980) reported the results of a victimization survey conducted in Vancouver, B.C., in 1979. They analyzed violent personal victimizations (sexual assaults, robbery, assault) and uncovered associations with age, sex, and marital status similar to those existing in the U.S. National Crime Survey data. In addition, they utilized a direct measure of out-of-home exposure: how many times a month the respondent went out during the evening for various activities. Corrado and his colleagues found that people whose frequency of going out during the evening was higher than the median frequency in the sample had a rate of violent personal victimization that was more than triple the rate of people whose frequency of going out was less than the median.

Because demographic variables (such as age, sex, and marital status) are indirect indicators of various aspects of lifestyle (such as frequency of going out), Corrado and his colleagues hypothesized that the associations between the demographic variables and victimization would disappear, or at least be attenuated, once frequency of going out was taken into account. This apparently did not occur. Associations between victimizations and sex and age continued to exist among persons with high (above the median) scores on the "nights out" variable as well as among persons with low (below the median) scores. However, it must be remembered that frequency of going out in the evening is only one aspect of lifestyle on which people in various age, sex, and marital status categories differ. Furthermore, an overall measure of the frequency of going out in the evening does not take into account the different types of activities in which people engage while they are out. The importance of types of activities is evident in the results of the next study to be discussed.

Using victimization survey data from residents of a community in the Midlands of England, Smith (1982) found that a number of lifestyle-relevant variables (e.g., age, social class) discriminated victims from nonvictims. More important here, however, is Smith's variable reflecting frequency of spare-time activities, which she found to be the most powerful predictor of victimization.

Carrying the analysis a step further, Smith looked at the proportions of victims and nonvictims who reported engaging in different types of spare-time activities. For activities that are generally structured and that involve associating primarily with friends or relatives—that is, organized clubs, religious meetings, visiting family and friends, education—the differences between the percentages of victims and nonvictims reporting participation were slight. But large differences were evident for activities that are less structured and that involve more contact with strangers in public places. For example, 29% of the nonvictims, but 40% of the victims, reported participation in "cinema/theater/dancing/bingo" as a spare-time activity. Likewise, 18% of the nonvictims, but 34% of the victims, reported "frequenting pubs/cafes" as a spare-time activity (Smith, 1982: 393).

Preliminary findings from two more recent, large-scale victimization survey programs provide additional support for lifestyle models. Data from the British Crime Survey (Hough and Mayhew, 1983) show that violent victimization is positively associated with frequency of going out in the evening and with drinking habits, particularly among people between 16 and 30 years old. The 1982 Canadian victimization survey, conducted in several urban areas, found that respondents' average number of evening activities outside the home per month was associated positively with rates of robbery, assault, personal theft, and, to a lesser extent, sexual assault.

Areal Studies

There are several other lines of research that have produced findings relevant to lifestyle-type models of victimization. For example, the whole body of work dealing with areal variations in crime patterns is important to the notion that spatial proximity to potential offenders increases the likelihood of victimization. Because areal studies have such a long history and are so numerous, it is impossible to review even the major findings in this presentation. For my present purpose, it will be sufficient to note two recent studies that illustrate how some areal findings are directly relevant to lifestyle issues while others may not be.

Roncek (1981) reported associations between official crime counts and aggregate characteristics at the block level for two U.S. cities: Cleveland, Ohio and San Diego, California. In both cities, he found that rates of violent and property crimes were positively associated with the concentration of apartment housing and the concentration of "primary individuals" (the percentage of households with no relatives of the head of household present) on city blocks. These indicators reflect urban areas in which unmarried, unattached persons are concentrated in a type of housing that minimizes recognition of and interactions with neighbors. One can also infer that the indicators describe areas in which households are frequently left unattended while the occupants are out pursuing occupational and leisure interests. Thus the indicators represent residential concentration of particular lifestyles, and it is often the case that people choose to live in these neighborhoods because these neighborhoods are consistent with their lifestyles.

More typical of findings in areal research are those uncovered by Sampson and Castellano (1982) who utilized the "neighborhood characteristics" information that appears on the National Crime Survey data tapes. They found strong negative associations between the economic status of neighborhoods (measured either by median income or the unemployment rate) and rates of personal crime in the central cities of U.S. metropolitan areas. This oft-reported finding illustrates the heightened risk of victimization faced by people who reside in neighborhoods that have high concentrations of potential offenders. However, it is questionable to treat this finding as evidence of an association between lifestyle and victimization risk. Economic (and racial) segregation among urban neighborhoods is really a structural feature of a given society. Certainly, the limited residential options available to low-income and minority group members represent a structural constraint that influences their life opportunities, but the fact of being constrained to live—because of low income or racial/ethnic characteristics—in a high-crime neighborhood is not, in itself, an aspect of people's routine daily vocational and leisure activities. In contrast, when one has options of where to live and chooses to live in a neighborhood having features that are consistent with one's style of life—as I inferred was reflected in the Roneck findings discussed above—the ramifications of that choice for the risk of being victimized can be treated as being a product of lifestyle.

The difference in the relevance of the two areal studies to the lifestyle model of victimization represents an issue that is basic in conceptualizing and testing the model: Which features of a person's total life situation should be subsumed under the concept of lifestyle? Lines must be drawn somewhere. If lifestyle refers to any and all aspects of people's life situations, then the criticism mentioned earlier is valid: Any association can be incorporated into the model in an *ex post facto* fashion, and the theory represented by the model is nonfalsifiable. I will deal with this issue later, when some modifications of the lifestyle model are suggested. But now we can turn to another body of evidence that is relevant to the lifestyle model.

Studies of Offenders

A central hypothesis of the lifestyle model is that, given the disproportionate contact among persons who share similar lifestyles and the importance of demographic characteristics as indicators of lifestyle difference, "an individual's chances of personal victimization are dependent upon the extent to which the individual shares demographic characteristics with offenders" (Hindelang et al., 1978: 257). Therefore, to be consistent with the lifestyle model, studies of offenders should show that people who are involved disproportionately in the commission of personal crimes have demographic characteristics similar to people who are disproportionately the victims of personal crimes. Furthermore, these results should be present in studies that do not rely on data about only those offenders who have become enmeshed in the criminal justice system (e.g., self-reports of offenders and victims). In general, the findings are consistent with the lifestyle model.

Studies using victim perceptions of offender characteristics in the National Crime Survey show that rates of offending are higher among males than among females, and that they are particularly high among young black males (Hindelang, 1978, 1981)—the same demographic groups with the highest victimization rates for personal crimes. Focusing on offender age groups, McDermott (1979) found that, in personal crimes, juvenile offenders predominantly chose other juveniles as their victims, while adult offenders predominantly chose other adults. Even in the relatively small subset of personal crimes committed by female offenders, Young (1979) found that the majority of victims were female, and the victims and offenders generally fell into the same age group.

Additional evidence appears in recent analyses of self-report and official data from follow-up research on a sample of subjects who were identified in the initial study of delinquency in a Philadelphia birth cohort (Wolfgang et al., 1972). For example, Thornberry and Farnworth (1982) found that social status was negatively associated with criminal involvement among white and black male adults in the sample. Perhaps the most compelling evidence from this data source appears in Singer's (1981) description of "homogeneous victim-offender populations." Not only did he find that those who were most likely to report being the victims of serious assaultive violence had characteristics similar to offenders in these crimes (e.g., unemployed, single, black, school dropouts), but also that the same people often alternate between being victims and offenders in serious assaultive violence. Victims of these crimes showed higher levels of involvement in both official and self-reported criminal activity than did others; they were also more likely to have a friend who had been arrested and to have a history of gang membership.

Singer's findings are consistent with the preliminary findings of the British Crime Survey (Hough and Mayhew, 1983). In this survey, there was a relatively strong association between self-reported offending and being the victim of a violent offense.

There are other types of studies of offenders that produce evidence relevant to a lifestyle model of victimization. For example, research on offender mobility and target selection techniques (e.g., Carter and Hill, 1979) can help us understand why particular lifestyles are associated with higher than average risks of victimization. But, as was the case with areal studies of crime, the volume of research on offenders is much too great to be reviewed here.

Before closing this brief review of recent research, it should be noted that the number of countries in which victimization survey data are becoming available is increasing (see, for example, Steinmetz, 1979; Sveri, 1982; Corrado et al., 1980; Braithwaite and Biles, 1980; Hough and Mayhew, 1983; Solicitor General of Canada, 1983). This will allow lifestyle-type models to be subjected to the most rigorous type of testing—namely, whether they can stand up to cross-cultural examination.

In sum, a variety of types of studies reported since the lifestyle model was published in 1978 have generated findings that are consistent with the lifestyle model. However, some findings suggest ways in which the model should be modified.

MODIFYING THE LIFESTYLE MODEL

Figure 2.2 illustrates how the lifestyle model can be modified to provide a more thorough understanding of the risk of victimization. Before describing how and why Figure 2.2 differs from Figure 2.1, three comments are necessary. First, the model is meant to apply to "direct-contact predatory violations," as defined by Cohen and Felson (1979a). That is, the model is restricted to those types of crimes in which the offender comes into direct physical contact with the person or object that the offender wishes to injure or steal (or steal from). Although a number of crime types (e.g., corporate crimes) are excluded from consideration, "direct-contact predatory violations" covers more types of crime than the "personal crimes" used in the development of the original lifestyle model. Second, the actual workings of the model can vary depending on the nature of different crime types; for example, "associations" are less important for explaining variations in the risk of burglary than for explaining variations in the risk of robbery, while the opposite is probably true for "target attractiveness." Third, the model assumes given levels of offender motivation and state-provided protection from crime. These factors produce a certain level of crime potential, while variation in the elements shown in Figure 2.2 allow this potential to be realized to a greater or lesser extent.

The core of the original lifestyle model from Figure 2.1 remains: Lifestyles are formed through adaptations to role expectations and structural constraints, and different lifestyles embody different types of associations and levels of exposure, which affect the risk of victimization. But, in Figure 2.2, structural constraints are shown as having effects on associations and exposure that are not mediated through lifestyle. Primarily, this is meant to reflect the constraints of the

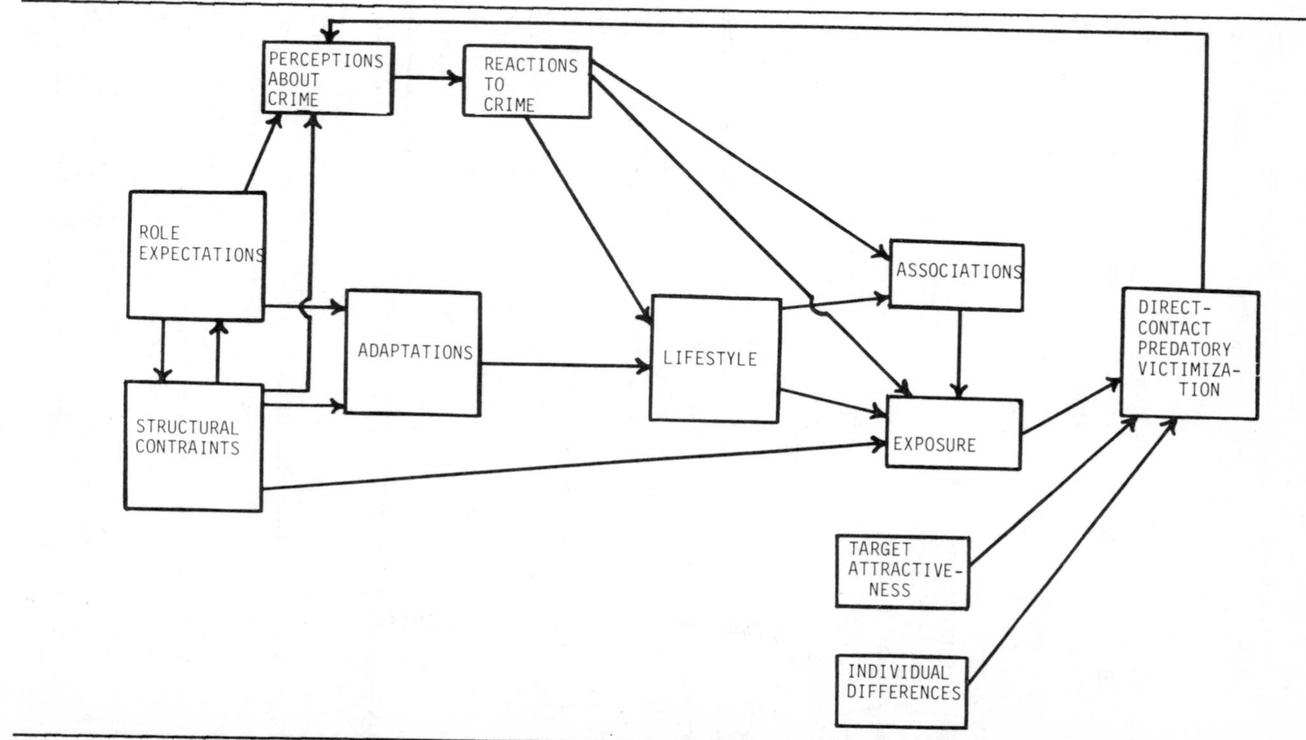

Figure 2.2 Modified Lifestyle Model for Direct-Contact, Predatory Victimization

economic system and the housing market on where people live. People who have sufficient economic resources and who are not constrained by racial/ethnic biases in the housing market can select their residences to fit their preferred style of living—for example, a rural setting, a singles apartment complex, a walled community with access controlled by security guards. The housing choices of these people can still have higher or lower risks of victimization depending on the patterns of their routine vocational and leisure activities. But the base level of risk that they face is heightened by their sheer proximity—and hence exposure—to potential offenders.

Another modification involves the inclusion of "reactions to crime" as a factor that affects exposure and associations both directly and through lifestyle. Reactions to crime represent the behavioral manifestations of perceptions about crime (e.g., fear, evaluation of risk, belief about the amount and nature of crime) that can stem from a variety of sources not shown in the model (e.g., the media) as well as from the first-hand experience of being victimized, indicated by the feedback loop in Figure 2.2 (see Garofalo, 1981; Skogan and Maxfield, 1981). Reactions to crime can involve relatively minor changes in what people do, such as selecting a bar frequented by fewer unsavory characters, buying better locks, or avoiding dimly lit streets when walking home at night. In these cases, the reactions have direct effects on associations and exposure. However, reactions to crime can also be far-reaching and involve basic changes in how one spends one's time. Examples would be deciding never to go out in the evening unaccompanied or foregoing access to the cultural amenities of a large city in order to move to the relative safety of a distant suburb. Such major reactions affect associations and exposure via basic changes in one's lifestyle.

Finally, two factors unrelated to lifestyle are shown as having direct effects on the risk of victimization: target attractiveness and individual differences. No attempt has been made to develop ideas about what variables influence target attractiveness or individual differences or to show how these factors might interrelate with the rest of the model. This is because the boxes labeled "target attractiveness" and "individual differences" in Figure 2.2 really represent undeveloped models that should be worked out somewhat independently before they can be fully linked with the lifestyle model.

Target attractiveness, for example, includes notions about offender perceptions, and it involves symbolic as well as instrumental considerations. In the instrumental realm, we may be able to assign some objective dollar worth to a potential target, but an offender's instrumental valuation of a potential target may involve unique considerations: for example, the desirability of the target for personal use or for use by one's friends, or the particular types of property that are most easily disposed of through the channels to which the offender has access. Furthermore, the target may have little instrumental significance to the offender, but a great deal of symbolic significance; for example, selection of a target for the vandal's destructiveness or the assaulter's blows is likely to depend on the expressive needs of the offender, making target attractiveness a very subjective matter.

As it is used in Figure 2.2, target attractiveness reflects only the instrumental or symbolic "worth" of the target to the offender. It does not include the notions that some targets are more attractive because they are geographically closer or unguarded; these factors are included within the concept of exposure. Thus a full explication of target attractiveness would require a model of the perceptions and judgments of offenders.

The box labeled "individual differences" in Figure 2.2 also represents an unexplicated model. Its inclusion is meant to signify that variations in risk cannot be accounted for entirely at the sociological level of explanation; psychological and even biological variables may be relevant. For example, people differ in their psychological propensities toward risk-taking and in the images of physical vulnerability that they project to potential offenders. These characteristics are best treated as individual-level variables, while lifestyle, as noted earlier, refers to regular patterns of behaviors among population aggregates. The model implied by the box labeled "individual differences" pertains to potential victims, but at a different level of explanation than the notion of lifestyle.

Inclusion of target attractiveness and individual differences as factors in Figure 2.2 is meant to illustrate that the risk of victimization cannot be understood fully without considering offenders and nonsociological levels of explanation. But my major purpose in Figure 2.2 has been to incorporate perceptions about/reactions to crime and the unmediated effects of structural constraints (primarily residential location) into the lifestyle model. By doing so, I believe that the lifestyle model comes into sharper focus, particularly because there is less of a temptation to expand the lifestyle concept into areas where it does not belong. For example, the fact that poor people and minority group members are constrained to live in high-crime areas of cities is important in determining their exposure to potential criminals; but it is preferable to treat that constraint separately in the model rather than to try to force economic/racial housing segregation into a concept that is defined as the patterning of routine vocational and leisure activities. Likewise, the addition of unmediated effects of reactions to crime on associations and exposure frees one from the temptation to dilute the lifestyle concept by forcing into it relatively narrow behaviors, such as locking doors and windows.

POLICY IMPLICATIONS OF THE MODEL

In discussions with others about lifestyle-type models of victimization, I occasionally hear the complaint: "That's all very neat in an academic sort of way, but it says nothing about how we should go about reducing the risk of victimization. What are we to do? Tell people to change their lifestyles?"

Such reactions miss a very important point in the lifestyle model: Namely, that lifestyles are shaped by social forces, designated as role expectations and structural constraints in the model. And the fact is that both role expectations and structural constraints—and, therefore, lifestyles—are influenced by public policies. For example, tax policies and legal provisions that encourage or discourage marriage or divorce influence the proportion of households that consist of unattached persons living alone; public subsidies for highways and other forms of transportation encourage mobility in the population; primary dependence on the free market for housing encourages the segregation of residential areas; mandatory school attendance, restrictions on the participation of the young in the labor force, and mandatory retirement ages discourage associations across age groups; subsidies for the refurbishing of inner-city housing encourage the movement of upper-middle-class households into relatively high-crime neighborhoods; vigorous enforcement of affirmative action programs can draw more women into the labor force; various economic policies affect the level of unemployment. The list could be extended, but I don't believe it is necessary to do so.

In reading through the preceding list, it should be obvious that some of the public policies than encourage lifestyles associated with *higher* risks of victimization are *not* policies that many of us would want to do away with. A good example is affirmative action programs for women.

The lifestyle model predicts that, as more women leave housekeeping roles and assume the roles of employees (or unemployed) persons, the risk of victimization for women should increase. But this is certainly not a reason to restrict the opportunities for women to enter the labor force. The potential positive and negative effects of other policies may be less clear. For example, encouraging more interaction across age groups in the labor force and in other spheres of life may decrease the risk of victimization for young people and increase the risk for older people as the associations of members of each group become less age-homogeneous. At the same time, elimination of policies such as mandatory school attendance, restriction on child labor, and mandatory retirement could lead, in some economies, to the exploitation of both groups in the labor market.

Thus it is clear that public policies can affect lifestyles and risks of victimization. It is not always clear what the effect will be, nor is it certain that a possible negative effect on the risk of victimization would outweigh other positive effects of a policy. In fact, it is quite reasonable to argue that increased risk of criminal victimization is a logical accompaniment of increases in the material wealth and personal freedom of a society—particularly if the increases in wealth and freedom are distributed unequally in the population.

My argument is not for or against any particular policy; rather, it is that implications for the risk of victimization should be taken into account as costs or benefits when policies are considered. Furthermore, recognition of these implications could make it possible to anticipate and try to deal with increases in victimization risks that might accompany the implementation of otherwise positive policies. At the very least, an understanding of how variations in crime are interrelated with variations in patterns of legitimate behavior should temper the urge to offer simplistic, one-sided "explanations" of crime.

CLOSING REMARKS

Our understanding of crime has been enhanced, during the past decade, by looking beyond offender motivation and by examining the potential targets of crime and the contexts in which crime occur. The lifestyle model of victimization has contributed to this advancement. However, the tenets of positive criminology require that our theories and models not lay stagnant or become enshrined. Rather, theories and models should be assessed continually in light of accumulating evidence and conceptual critiques. If this occurs with open-minded rigor, eventually every theory or model will be superseded or transformed to the extent that its roots are no longer easily identifiable. The lifestyle model of victimization has not reached this point yet. The preceding pages have shown that the model is consistent with research conducted since it was first presented and that it is capable of being modified and expanded to take fresh insights into consideration.

Despite the fact that I was involved in the development of the lifestyle model, I recognize that it will not survive forever—nor should it. At some point, testing and reconceptualization will lead to the development of a new model or a full-blown integrated theory of victimization. As an adherent of positive criminology, I not only look forward to that day, I also hope to participate in bringing it about.

3

Sociological Positivism and the Explanation of Criminality

LAWRENCE E. COHEN
KENNETH C. LAND

Positivism stresses the idea that intellectual disciplines can progress only to the degree that their knowledge is grounded in facts and experience. This rigid form of empiricism asserts that propositions and explanations have no significance unless they have referents that can be observed through the scientific method (Hoult, 1974: 243-244). Positivistic criminology has encompassed a wide diversity of thinking on research in crime and images of criminals. For over 200 years, many biological, psychological, social, economic, and environmental factors have been identified as the main determinants of crime and delinquency by positivistic criminologists.

In this chapter, we review the major contemporary sociological positivistic theories of crime and delinquency, examining their causal structures and empirical adequacy. We then propose a synthesis of the most promising positivistic theory and the routine activity model, a model that falls outside the traditional positivistic emphasis on the offender. Our purpose is to improve our ability to explain and predict delinquent and criminal behavior.

Authors' Note: This research was supported, in part, by the National Science Foundation, Grant Number SES-8217865. We are indebted to Marcus Felson, James R. Kluegel, Michael R. Gottfredson, and David Cantor whose collaboration has led to the systematic development of the ideas presented.

CONTEMPORARY POSITIVISTIC SOCIOLOGICAL THEORIES OF CRIME AND DELINQUENCY

The major contemporary positivistic sociological approaches to crime and delinquency causation generally employ two contrasting analytic models in their explanations. One views the causes of crime in social disorganization, while the other believes the roots of this phenomenon to be in cultural deviance. According to Ruth Kornhauser's (1978: 21) authoritative text, social disorganization explains crime as resulting from lack of articulation of values within a culture or from lack of articulation between culture and social structure, while cultural deviance explains crimes as socialization to subcultural values and norms that conflict with established criminal law.

For example, all social disorganization models share the assumption of common societal values that are enacted into criminal law and perceive crime as the violation of laws that results when one's commitment to conformity is weak or nonexistent. According to Kornhauser (1978: 24), common to all social disorganization theories is the notion that "crime is produced by malfunctioning social structures, malintegrated cultures or faulty links between the two." More specifically, social disorganization theories contend that

> the intervening causes of delinquency are in varying pressures (strains) or constraints (controls) resulting from varying degrees of social disorganization. Candidates for delinquency are socially selected from incumbents of social positions burdened with undue strain, or from those isolated from controlling social bonds [Kornhauser, 1978: 24].

Thus, according to Kornhauser, there are two variants of social disorganization theory—one a strain model (e.g., Merton, 1938; Cohen, 1955; Cloward and Ohlin, 1960), the other a control model (e.g., Thrasher, 1927; Shaw and McKay, 1929; Hirschi, 1969). The strain model specifies the causes of crime and delinquency to be structurally induced frustration resulting from the discrepancy between aspirations and expectations. The control model, on the other hand, assumes the pressure to deviate from conventional norms to be relatively constant across individuals. The control theorists see crime and delinquency to be most likely perpetrated by those who are least constrained by internal control (i.e., guilt, shame, or stakes in conformity). To a lesser extent, control theorists have also identified external controls (i.e., surveillance, supervision) as barriers to crime and delinquency. Of particular interest to control theorists are a person's bonds to family, community, school, or job that are the source of personal costs of criminal behavior (Kornhauser, 1978: 24-25).

Cultural deviance theorists (e.g., Sutherland, 1939; Miller, 1958; Sellin, 1938) view criminal behavior as conformity to a set of subcultural standards that are in opposition to the accepted legal norms of the larger more powerful cultural order. Crime is thus a product of differentiated societies.

Although several theorists (e.g., Shaw and McKay, 1929; Cloward and Ohlin, 1960; Cohen, 1955) have offered theories of crime or delinquency causation that combine control or strain models of social disorganization with cultural deviance models, they are best classified into the above categories for the purpose of identifying their respective analytical models. Insofar as a theory treats a criminal subculture as an independent variable generating criminal behavior based on a process of socialization, it is classified as a cultural deviance model. But if the criminal subculture is viewed as a dependent variable, surviving only in the process of social disorganization and dependent on the supply of recruits through exogenous factors, the theory is classified as a social disorganization model (Kornhauser, 1978: 26).

Research testing the empirical adequacy of cultural deviance, strain, and control models has been most supportive of the latter. Of course, much of the data gathered to test these respective models has been obtained from responses to questionnaires and interviews. Values, attitudes, and beliefs are often better measured from deeds than from words. What people actually do or feel may be poorly measured by what they say. With this caveat in mind, let us review the empirical evidence gathered to evaluate the adequacy of cultural deviance, strain, and control models of criminal and delinquent behavior.

Cultural deviance models presume extensive disagreement in the evaluations of crime among various subgroups of American society. Yet all existing surveys reveal considerable consensus in evaluations of crime among various subgroups, despite the fact that Index Crime (murder, forcible rape, aggravated assault, robbery, burglary, larceny-theft, motor vehicle theft) and delinquency rates are known to vary substantially among these groups (Michael, 1963; Maccoby et al., 1958; Conklin, 1971; Rossi et al., 1974; Thomas, 1976). Related evidence further demonstrates that the degree of value agreement among subgroups in the U.S. population regarding the use of violence, as well as attitudes toward police protection run counter to the predictions of cultural deviance theory (Ball-Rokeach, 1973; Blumenthal et al., 1972; Almond and Verba, 1963; Miller and Roby, 1970). In addition, there is evidence that delinquents and criminals do not approve of their own illegal conduct (Sechrest, 1969; Matza, 1964; Buffalo and Rogers, 1971); that the "delinquent subculture" does not contain a set of inverse values (Gold, 1963); and that delinquents affirm, rather than condemn, conventional (middle-class) standards of morality (Short and Strodbeck, 1965; Gordon et al., 1963; Lerman, 1968; Hirschi, 1969). Finally, there is some evidence that the temporal position of associations with delinquents and criminals in the crime causation process might be opposite to that implied by cultural deviance theories (Elliot and Voss, 1974).

Much of the accumulated empirical evidence also runs counter to the claims of strain theory. One of the basic arguments of strain theory is that those with high aspirations but low expectations of achievement will have the highest probability of engaging in crime and delinquency. However, data collected to test this assumption consistently indicate that the highest rates of illegal activity occur among those with low aspirations and low expectations (Short et al., 1965; Hirschi, 1969). Other evidence indicates that aspirations are not uniformly high across the social classes (Hyman, 1953); that status frustration (as measured by anticipated failure to achieve culturally prescribed goals of success) is not related to rates of self-reported delinquency (Elliot and Voss, 1974); and that occupational aspirations of delinquents appear to be as optimistic as those of nondelinquents (Gold, 1963; Fredericks and Molner, 1969).

Relative to cultural deviance and strain models, the empirical evidence appears to be more supportive of social control theory. Jensen and Rojeck (1980: 179), after reviewing much of this evidence, note that one argument for which control theory seems to have received considerable support is the contention that studying the strength of barriers against crime is more useful than studying motivation to commit crime (see also Matza, 1964; Gold, 1970). This they feel downplays the role of motivational factors and emphasizes the situational nature of much crime and delinquency.

Other research focusing on barriers to crime and delinquency constantly indicates that there is a significant relationship between attachments to conventional others, values, and institutions, as well as one's stake in conformity and delinquent behavior. For example, studies by Hirschi (1969), Jensen (1972), Hindelang (1973), Hepburn (1976), and Wiatrowski et al. (1981) all suggest that young people who are sensitive to and concerned with the opinions of parents and teachers, those who aspire to high educational and vocational status, and those who believe most in the moral validity of the law engage in fewer delinquencies than do those with fewer stakes in conformity.

Among the major contemporary positivistic sociological theories of crime causation, the propositions of control theory appear to be more consistent with the empirical evidence than are those of cultural deviance or strain theory. After thorough and analytical review of the above theories, Kornhauser (1978: 253) concludes that the field should now turn to "the more definitive formation of control models, to the more adequate linking to macrosocial and microsocial control theories, and to their more rigorous testing." Adherents of cultural deviance and strain models will disagree with Kornhauser's assessment, and there may be some reason for their concern. Empirical tests of the validity of the propositions implied by each of these three analytic models generally have considered only cross-sectional variations in the distribution of crime—across cities, states, socioeconomic groups, or nations, rather than variations over time in any one place or collection of places. As we will see in the next section, however, longitudinal research does not save strain or cultural deviance models. Indeed, the ability of the three contemporary positivistic theories to account for both crime trends and distributions in the post-World War II United States is questionable.

THEORETICAL INADEQUACIES OF EXPLANATIONS OF CRIME TRENDS

The three theoretical models discussed above have generally been empirically evaluated using cross-sectional data. Can cross-sectional analyses of crime rates be used to draw inferences about the causes of crime? More generally, can cross-sectional relationships be used to make inferences about the causes of any social phenomena? An increasing body of theoretical and empirical literature argues that the answer to this question is no (but see Hirschi and Gottfredson, 1983). In a comparison of dynamic and static mathematical models of relationships among variables, Coleman (1968: 444) pointed out the rather stringent aggregate equilibrium assumptions necessary to make inferences about a dynamic social process from cross-sectional relationships. Substantive studies in which these assumptions apparently do not hold are not difficult to find. In the study of mother-tongue diversity in nations, for example, Lieberson and colleagues (Lieberson and Hansen, 1974;

Lieberson et al., 1975) presented longitudinal findings that clearly contradict cross-national patterns.

With respect to the study of crime, the National Commission on the Causes and Prevention of Violence (1969), Wilson (1975), and Cohen and Felson (1979b) have all pointed out that the trends in many of the presumed causal variables in contemporary positivistic sociological theories are in directions opposite to those necessary to account for crime trends on the basis of conventional cross-sectional relationships.

The three types of positivistic criminological theory we have reviewed above stress two separate images of the criminal. Control theorists see the offender as a relatively undersocialized person whose conscience is weakened by the absence of internal controls and whose bond to society is not developed due to inadequate controls over his or her behavior. Strain and cultural deviance theories, on the other hand, see the offender as a highly socialized person whose criminal behavior represents conformity to an ethical code that makes deviant conduct mandatory (Empey, 1982: 286). These theories have failed to account for a great deal of variance in rates of criminal behavior, both at the cross-sectional (see Johnson, 1979) and longitudinal levels of analysis (Cohen and Felson, 1979b), primarily because they focus entirely on motivation or social psychological constraints on behavior and ignore other elements necessary for the successful completion of a criminal act. In addition, these three theoretical models have not adequately interpreted how social and economic changes affect the rate of crime across and within social areas.

In the next section, we argue that when we extend the focus of crime beyond the usual concentration on criminal motivation or social psychological constraints to include other necessary theoretical ingredients for the successful completion of criminal acts, we obtain a model that is capable of accounting for both cross-sectional and longitudinal patterns of crime.

EXTENDING THE FOCUS OF CRIMINAL EXPLANATIONS BEYOND MOTIVATION

We believe that a broader, more systematic theoretical and empirical inquiry is needed. The model we offer as a first step in extending our focus beyond offender motivation or social psychological constraints is derived primarily from the lifestyle-exposure theoretical framework of

Hindelang et al. (1978), and the criminal opportunity perspective of the authors and their colleagues (Land and Felson, 1976; Cohen and Felson, 1979b; Cohen et al., 1980; Cohen et al., 1981).

The criminal opportunity theory developed by the authors and their colleagues has been used to explain both crime rate trends and social differentiation in the distribution of predatory criminal victimization. This theory is based upon a Durkheimian/human ecological conception of criminal acts as routine activities that feed upon other routine activities. In particular, it defines the class of direct-contact predatory crimes as violations that involve the concurrence in space and time of three conditions: the presence of motivated offenders, the presence of suitable targets, and the absence of effective guardians (Cohen and Felson, 1979b).

A criminal opportunity model for the explanation of crime trends concentrates on examining how social changes affect the concurrence of the above three conditions and focuses specifically on those social changes that might alter the concentration of sustenance and leisure activities within family households (Felson et al., 1978). A general theoretical proposition of this approach would suggest that any decrease in the concentration of activities within family-based households would increase crime rates. Thus any social change that has the affect of increasing the dispersion of activities outside those households that are made up of individuals related to each other by family ties would contribute to increases in predatory or index crime rates by exposing persons and/or their property to greater risk of criminal victimization (Felson et al., 1978). Cohen and Felson (1979b) suggest that increasing rates of female labor force participation and of formation of single-person households (or households consisting of unrelated individuals) by divorced persons, students, and other young adults are two of the major post-World War II social changes that have had the affect of dispersing sustenance and leisure activities outside the household.

ECONOMIC CHANGE AND CRIMINAL OPPORTUNITY

From the perspective of criminal opportunity theory, an expanding economy may contribute to rising crime rates insofar as this leads to a deconcentration of sustenance and leisure activities within family-based households. Indeed, the criminal opportunity approach sharply contrasts with many interpretations of how crime rates vary with levels of poverty and unemployment. For example, periods of high unemployment tend to keep people at home. In addition, an economic recession generally means less overtime work that reduces the necessity of traveling home on relatively unoccupied and dark streets. Also, people may have less discretionary income to spend on recreation outside their home or city, though they may spend more time engaged in activities in or near their homes. In brief, since periods of high unemployment, on the whole, probably are periods of greater concentration of sustenance and leisure activities within or near one's household, criminal opportunity theory implies that burglary, robbery, and other direct-contact predatory crime rates will vary inversely with unemployment rates. Thus the criminal opportunity approach would predict precisely the opposite relationship between temporal changes in the unemployment rate and crime rates from that reported by Brenner (1976a, 1976b) and others (see Felson et al., 1978).

A criminal opportunity perspective also suggests that prosperity will tend to increase rather than decrease rates of property crime by making more property available for theft. Furthermore, the economic improvement of the position of the lower strata in society may actually enhance property crime rates, for the members of these strata are more likely to live proximate to potential property offenders. Since offenders tend to find their targets relatively near to their own residence (Reiss, 1976) it follows that improvements in the economic position of the lower strata will tend to increase their risk of victimization and hence contribute to crimes.

CRIMINAL OPPORTUNITY AND CRIMINAL MOTIVATION

The question remains whether a criminal opportunity perspective is any more viable than traditional criminological theories in explaining crime rate trends. Previous studies by the authors and their colleagues indicate that it might be. The analysis of U.S. crime trends in the post-World War II United States by Cohen and Felson (1979b) indicate that some traditional theories have difficulty accounting for annual changes. However, a criminal opportunity approach enabled Cohen et al. (1980) to account accurately for and forecast burglary, robbery, and motor vehicle theft rates in the United States for the years 1947-1977.

As Felson et al. (1978: 21) note, "A criminal opportunity theory predicts that the dispersion of activities away from husband-wife households enables offenses to become more successful for their perpetrators, more costly to victims, and more intrusive into their personal space." Hence one might expect this dispersion to produce explosive growth not only in the occurrence but also in the reporting of direct-contact predatory violations. While initial tests of this theoretical perspective concentrated on macro-level analyses over time, recent cross-sectional tests with micro-level data have also offered strong support for this perspective (Cohen and Cantor, 1980, 1981; Cohen et al., 1981a, 1981b; Hindelang et al., 1978).

One important and distinctive aspect of this recent line of research on criminal opportunities is that it has achieved general consistency with the data about crime and victimization without explicit references to what motivates people to commit crimes. Implicit in the model is, of course, a concept of offender motivation—one that sees motivation at least partially caused by the lack of external physical restraints. The absence of capable guardians and the presence of suitable targets allow motivated offenders to exercise their criminal inclinations. Motivation to crime is taken as nonproblematic, the task being to predict the situations in which criminal inclinations are translated into action—the translation being provided by the *absence* of ordinary physical restraints such as the presence of other people or objects that inhibit, or are perceived to inhibit, the successful completion of direct contact predatory crime. Hence this perspective explicitly focuses away from offender motivation. It assumes a pool of motivated offenders and examines the manner in which the spatial and temporal organization of social activities help people to translate their criminal inclination into action.

Clearly, the criminal opportunity perspective is not the first crime causation perspective to question the empirical necessity to posit motivation differences as the main key to understanding crime rates. Such a stance has long been associated with sociological theories of control (Hirschi, 1969). In sociological versions of control theory it is rather assumed that (a) all people are strongly motivated to satisfy their needs and wants, (b) some of these needs and wants can be satisfied by criminal behavior, and (c) there exists variability in the constraints that prohibit the attempt to satisfy needs and wants through illegal activities. The prospects are obviously good for merging control and opportunity theories.

SYNTHESIZING CONTROL AND OPPORTUNITY THEORIES

The propositions of control theory are more consistent with empirical evidence than are those of cultural deviance or strain theory. We believe that the concepts of control theory also provide the basis for a fruitful synthesis of the control and criminal opportunity approach to the explanation of crime. The key to this synthesis lies in the recognition that both these theories incorporate, explicitly or implicitly, notions of internal or external controls, but differ as to whether these controls are conceived of as having been primarily accumulated in the past socialization experiences and associations or effectively operating in the present situation.

Control theory views the likely offender as an undersocialized person unconstrained by internal or external controls; controls primarily accumulated in the past, which the individual brings with him or her into the situation where a criminal act is possible.

Criminal opportunity theory also emphasizes the role of certain external controls—those that are largely physical and situationally present in determining rates of offending within communities. This perspective argues that structural differentials and/or changes in routine activity patterns can influence crime rates and/or trends by affecting the spatio-temporal convergence of the three minimal elements of direct-contact predatory crimes: motivated offenders, suitable targets, and the absence of effective guardians. The lack of any one of these three physical elements is seen as situationally sufficient to prevent the successful completion of crimes. Control, therefore, is also critical to criminal opportunity theory. If controls over opportunities for crimes (i.e., control factors that affect suitable targets or capable guardians) decrease, the theory predicts that illegal predatory acts will increase.

It appears social control theories primarily emphasize the heritage of past experiences, associations, and socialization that the individual brings to the criminal situation, while the criminal opportunity approach emphasizes physical controls that are perceived to be, or are actually situationally present (or absent, depending on one's point of view) when a crime is committed. We are interested in the possible consequences of merging the control and opportunity perspectives. We believe that such a synthesis may yield a more powerful explanation of crime causation than that which results when each is considered independently.

A merging of social control and opportunity perspectives may prove useful in explaining why the criminal justice system, the community, and the family now appear relatively ineffective in exerting social control compared to earlier periods in American history. Substantial increases in the opportunity to carry out predatory violations may have undermined society's mechanism for social control. For example, it may be difficult for institutions seeking to increase the certainty, severity, and celerity of punishment to compete with structural changes resulting in vast increases in the certainty, celerity, and value of rewards obtained from illegal acts (Cohen and Felson, 1979b). Furthermore, the same structural changes that have increased the opportunity for and attractiveness of crime have also affected barriers to crime. Changes in the structure of sustenance and leisure activities have affected socialization processes, and the supervision and surveillance of potential offenders, and they have increased the opportunity for crime. Increases in female labor force participation, college enrollments, urbanization, transportation and highways, automobiles, and home appliances provide opportunities to escape the confines of the household, while at the same time increasing the risk of victimization or offending by removing people from potential guardians and supervisors, thus weakening social control (Cohen and Felson, 1979b).

Still another body of evidence attesting to the potential of merging social control and opportunity perspectives demonstrates that the factors most closely associated with victimization are the very factors that are also most strongly correlated with the probability of offending (Hindelang et al., 1978; Cohen et al., 1981a). Virtually all sources of data agree that those involved most heavily in Index Crimes are disproportionately young, male, urban, poor, nonwhite, and unmarried. Government surveys of victim characteristics clearly demonstrate that victims disproportionately share these same characteristics (for summaries of this evidence, see Hindelang et al., 1978). These findings suggest additional support for the contention that similar mechanisms are operating, not only to reduce restraints on offending, but to increase the probability that potential offenders and potential victims will come into direct contact more often than when such characteristics are not shared. This principle (called the principle of homogamy by Cohen et al., 1981a) does not necessarily suggest that these processes produce victims and offenders who are one and the same, although as Gottfredson (1981) notes, there are considerable data to indicate that this is frequently the case. Rather, we contend that similarities in lifestyle increase the probability that homogamous individuals will be in proximity of one another, making contact with one another more likely.

From the above discussion, it would seem that the merging of a perspective that emphasizes declines in the barriers to crime (control theory) with one that emphasizes increases in situations in which crimes are likely to be successfully completed (criminal opportunity theory) may lead to a greater understanding of the circumstances in which crime is most likely to thrive. One of the major objectives of future research should be to carry out and empirically evaluate this synthesis as systematically, formally, and thoroughly as possible.

CONCLUSION

After reviewing the causal structures and empirical adequacy of cultural deviance, strain, and control theories, we conclude that, of the three, control theory has amassed the strongest empirical support. However, none of the above theories appears to account for a great deal of variance in rates of criminal behavior in either cross-sectional or longitudinal research. We have suggested that extending the focus of research to include other elements (beyond offender motivation) that are necessary for successful completion of predatory criminal acts might produce a model that is more adequate in accounting for both cross-sectional and longitudinal patterns of crime.

In this chapter, we have sketched how control and opportunity theories can be combined in order to gain a more inclusive model for the study of crime. However, this is only a first step. Both control and opportunity theories incorporate, explicitly or implicitly, notions of internal or external controls, but differ as to whether these controls are conceived as being largely internal and having been primarily accumulated in the past (control theory) or largely external and effectively operating in the present situation (opportunity theory). To this model, one may add expectations about the future as a determinant of crime. Deterrence theory, for example, unlike control and opportunity theories, largely ignores past and present internal or external controls and emphasizes the role of possible future (i.e., expected) punishments, administered by agents of the state, as increasing or decreasing the likelihood of crime. This perspective assumes that people behave rationally and are motivated to commit crime only after calculating the expected costs against the expected benefits of law breaking. Deterrence theorists thus propose that the greater the perceived costs of crime (i.e., the certainty, celerity, and severity of punishment), the lower the level of crime. Consequently, this perspective can also be viewed as an extension of control theory that emphasizes the role of external punishments by the state as the major control over crime.

It is possible that the merging of deterrence theory (which emphasizes controls that operate through expectations about the future) and criminal opportunity theory (which emphasizes situationally present or absent controls) with sociological control theory (which emphasizes the heritage of past experiences, associations, and socialization that the individual brings to such situations) is a promising avenue of development of a model that improves our ability to predict and explain criminal and delinquent behavior beyond our current capabilities.

4

Data for Positive Criminology

JOHN H. LAUB

Criminology has developed remarkably over the last fifteen years. One important result has been an explosion of research activity, a good portion of it of an interdisciplinary nature, which has rapidly expanded the knowledge base. Accompanying this change, there has been a powerful resurgence of what can be called *positive criminology*.

Positive criminology can be described by three attributes. First, positive criminology is characterized by the search to discover, in a statistical sense, the causes of criminal and delinquent behavior (Hirschi and Selvin, 1973: 38). The scientific method is utilized to differentiate offenders from nonoffenders on a variety of characteristics. The methodology of positive criminology assumes that there are identifiable factors that make people act as they do (determinism) and that the variability to be explained is associated with the variability in the causal agents (differentiation) (Gottfredson, 1982: 30).

Second, positive criminology can be depicted as an optimistic venture. This is not to say that positivist criminologists are more optimistic about the world than are antipositivists. Rather it is to say that positivist criminologists believe that using the scientific method is more likely to lead to answers to theoretical questions than hunches, guesses, or groundless speculations. Also, positive criminology is constantly moving forward by accumulating more and more knowledge, thereby increasing our ability to understand crime and delinquency.

Third, positive science can also be seen as a tool for "debunking" (Gould, 1981: 321). Here the goal of positive criminology is to shatter myths and to shed light on mistaken beliefs. Perhaps more than other disciplines, criminology often operates on the basis of conventional wisdom and gut-level knowledge. Positive criminology can counteract (but sometimes support) these tendencies by providing current research information to policymakers and the public. Therefore, positive criminology not only advances the state of the field by adding knowledge but also by replacing it. As Gould (1981: 322, emphasis in orginal) notes, "Scientists do not debunk only to cleanse and purge. They refute older ideas *in the light of* a different view about the nature of things."

The resurgence of positive criminology is in good part due to the work of Michael Hindelang. This essay in particular owes its existence to Michael's creative work with victimization survey data. Most criminological research on the correlates of offending has relied on official crime statistics, such as the Uniform Crime Reports (UCR), or on self-reports from individuals in the general population regarding their offending behavior. Recently, a third source of data, namely, victimization survey data, has been used to analyze the correlates of offending. This essay presents new analyses of the trends and patterns of offending in personal crimes using these victim-oriented data and compares the strengths and weaknesses of this approach to other data sources.

DATA FOR POSITIVE CRIMINOLOGY

The development of sound criminological theory depends upon the accurate identification of crime correlates. Indeed, Blalock (1970: 74) has stated that "in a very real sense the advancement of any science depends on the adequacy of its measurement procedures." Criminologists have traditionally used either data on arrests or self-reports of offenders to study the demographic correlates of offending, although numerous criticisms have been offered regarding the adequacy of these measurements of crime. One disadvantage of arrest data is that information is collected only on those crimes that are reported to the police, and it may be that those crimes exhibit characteristics that are different from the criminal events that are not reported to official authorities. More precisely, there is reason to be concerned that the police may be biased in their arrest policies toward certain groups, particularly those with limited economic and political power (e.g., young black males). If so, these groups would exhibit higher rates of "offending" compared with the general population because of differential handling by the police (Chambliss and Seidman, 1971). Differences may arise then as to age, race, and sex of offenders depending on what data source one uses. In addition, official crime statistics contain information only on offenses that are discovered, reported to proper authorities, and recorded by those authorities (Hindelang, 1974: 2).

Self-report data were designed, in part, to eliminate some of the weaknesses of official records noted above. These data, which are generated from surveys of the general population, focus on the offender's behavior, not the official justice system response. Therefore, it is believed that self-report data more accurately reflect the true distribution of criminal behavior.

However, the self-report data that have been collected suffer from two severe limitations. First, generally very small, nonrepresentative samples have been studied. As a result, complete information on age, race, and sex of offenders is lacking. Second, given the statistical rarity of serious crime across the United States, and because of the small sample sizes used, generally few self-report studies have generated enough serious offenses for adequate analysis. The emphasis has been on relatively trivial events. Thus it has been difficult for researchers to assess the demographic correlates of offending in serious crimes using self-report data. In many ways then, self-report data have been of the same limited utility as official records (Nettler, 1978: 117).

Fortunately, there exists a third data source for our consideration—victimization data. Recently, the Bureau of Justice Statistics, in cooperation with the Bureau of the Census, has produced a large body of information about serious crimes in the United States. These data are generated by surveying very large probability samples of the general population in order to ascertain the nature and extent of criminal victimizations that may have been suffered by respondents. Although not designed specifically to assess offender characteristics, these retrospective surveys of victims of crime avoid many of the problems and limitations inherent in official and self-report data.

When survey respondents indicate that they have experienced a criminal victimization, they are asked a series of detailed questions relating to every aspect of the offense; exactly what happened, when and where the offense occurred, whether any injury or loss was suffered as a result of the offense, who was present during the offense, whether it was reported to the police, and what the victim perceived to be the offender's sex, race, and age group (see Laub, 1983a, 1983b).

On the basis of these limited offender data, it is possible to pose many important questions regarding the basic facts surrounding the offenses of various subgroups of offenders. For a variety of reasons (e.g., the potential biases in police data, the lack of serious crimes in typical self-report studies), victimization surveys are likely to provide more adequate answers to these questions than either self-report or arrest data. This is not to say, though, that the victimization survey results, as a source of data about offenders, are without problems (see section on data limitations below). However, in spite of these weaknesses, the NCS data hold potential that is not found in official or self-report data (Hindelang and McDermott, 1981).

THE NATIONAL CRIME SURVEY DATA

The data reported represent estimates of crimes occurring in the United States based on weighted sample data. It is possible to make these estimates because a probability sample of respondents was surveyed. The interview completion rate in the national sample is about 95% or more of those selected to be interviewed in any given period.

This chapter will be concerned with the personal crimes of rape, robbery, assault, and personal larceny (purse snatching and pocket picking). Although the survey also collects data on the household crimes of burglary, larceny from the household, and motor vehicle theft, these crimes will not be included here. The analysis reported below requires reports from victims regarding what transpired during the event—particularly regarding offender characteristics such as the perceived age of the offender, and hence only those crimes generally involving contact between victims and offenders will yield this information. The details about what happened during the event are gathered by means of personal interviews with the victims themselves.

Depending on whether one or more than one offender is reported by the victim to have been involved in the incident, victims are asked one of two series of questions relating to offender characteristics. If a lone offender victimized the respondent, that offender's characteristics are simply recorded. If more than one offender was involved it is, of course, possible to have offenders of different ages, races, and sexes. In general, the tables and figures use the age of the *oldest* of the multiple offenders. Preliminary analysis shows that more often than not multiple offenders fall into the same age group; for this reason, whether the age of the youngest or the age of the oldest of the multiple offenders is used has little impact on the results (see Laub, 1983a, 1983b, for more details).

Although the NCS data (like UCR data) are incapable of providing information on the number of *distinct* offenders involved in offenses suffered by different victims, NCS rates of offending attempt to take into account the total number of offenders in each sex-race-age subgroup theoretically subject to arrest for the offense as reported to survey interviewers (Hindelang and McDermott, 1981: 39-40). This unique weighting procedure is accomplished by taking into account the total number of offenders in each sex-race-age subgroup for each incident. For example, if one victim reports having been victimized by one white male adult and two white female juveniles and another victim reports having been victimized by one black female adult and one white male adult, the sex-race-age subtotals for thse victimizations would be two white male adults, two white female juveniles, and one black female adult. This subtotaling process continues across all incidents reported to survey interviewers and results in a total number of offenders for each sex-race-age subgroup. These subgroup totals serve as the numerators for the rates of offending reported in this section; the denominators are estimates of the number of persons in the *general* population (i.e., potential offenders) in each sex-race-age subgroup. These offender-weighted rates of offending are reported per 100,000 potential offenders.

AGE AND SEX OF OFFENDER

Previous analyses of official statistics, such as Uniform Crime Report (UCR) data, and self-reports of offenders and victims have generally shown males to have larger rates of offending than females. This appears to be especially true when examining serious offenses (see Cernkovich and Giordano, 1979; Hindelang et al., 1981: 137-155; Hindelang, 1979).

Data in Table 4.1 show the rates of offending in personal crimes by age and sex of offender. In all three groups for all types of crime, the rates of offending for males are substantially greater than the female rates. Second, in all but one instance for males the highest offending age group is 18 to 20, while for females it is 12 to 17 years old. For instance, for total personal crimes, the largest sex difference is found in the 18- to 20-year-old age group where the rate of offending for males is 15 times the female rate, while among adults the male to female ratio is similarly large, about 13:1. Among juvenile offenders, the ratio of the male to female offending rate is the smallest—about 5:1. Similar patterns are evident for robbery and aggravated assault. Incidentally, robbery shows the largest male-female ratios of any offense type. Overall, these cross-sectional data indicate that sex is indeed an important correlate of offending in personal crimes and the magnitude of the sex effect varies with the age of the offender.

TABLE 4.1 Estimated Rates of Offending (per 100,000 potential offenders in each population subgroup), by Age of Offender,[a] Sex of Offender, and Type of Crime, NCS National Data, 1973-1981 Aggregate[b]

Age and Sex of Offender	Type of Crime: Rape	Robbery	Aggravated Assault	Simple Assault	Personal Larceny	Total Personal Crimes
12 to 17[c]						
Male	171	3,599	2,949	5,923	827	13,471
Female	–	294	377	2,133	90	2,908
18 to 20						
Male	414	6,973	6,625	10,191	1,271	25,475
Female	–	213	371	1,046	138	1,773
21 or older						
Male	218	1,280	1,643	2,455	190	5,787
Female	–	48	117	235	38	440

a. Includes perceived age of lone and perceived age of oldest multiple offender.
b. Excluded are incidents (about 10% of the total) in which the victim did not know whether there was one or more than one offender and incidents involving offenders of "mixed" sexes.
c. The numerator of the rates of offending for 12- to 17-year-olds excludes incidents (about 1% of the total) in which the offender was perceived by the victim to be under 12 years of age. The denominator of the rate is the number of 12- to 17-year-olds in the general population.

The trend data from the NCS corroborate the cross-sectional patterns. The large differences by sex persist over the period of 1973-1981. Concerns that over the last decade females have become more heavily involved in criminal activity (see, e.g., Adler, 1975; Simon, 1975) are simply not supported by the NCS data.

Figure 4.1 presents rates of offending by age and sex of offender in total personal crimes from 1973 to 1981. These victimization survey data indicate that *juvenile* female offending has in fact *declined* over the period. The patterns for adult females are more variable, but generally show a slight *increase*. Among males, juveniles also show a generally steady decline in rates of offending, albeit much less than females—an overall decrease of about 10% during the period. Rates for youthful offenders show a similar overall decline. However, rates for adult male offenders reveal an overall increase for the nine-year period.

AGE AND RACE OF OFFENDER

In contrast to the data on sex, previous analyses of official data and self-report data concerning race have been inconsistent and confusing. Race has been found to be a strong correlate in analyses using official data (e.g., Wolfgang et al., 1972) and at best a weak correlate in analyses using self-report data (Gould, 1969; Hirschi, 1969). Analysis of victimization survey data has produced results generally consistent with official records (Hindelang, 1978). However, in a recent study, Hindelang et al. (1981: 180) write, "On the whole . . . we were unsuccessful in finding large black/white differences in self-report scores, at least in part because blacks failed to report known official offenses at a much higher rate than whites with the same offenses indicated on their police and court records."

The data in Table 4.2 display rates of offending in personal crimes by age and race of offender. Blacks in all three age groups have a rate of offending that is much higher than that for whites across all crime types. In total personal crimes, the ratio of the black rate of offending to the white rate is about 4.5:1. Interestingly, these patterns are not age dependent. The black-white ratios are particularly large for robbery and personal larceny. Comparable to the data on sex, these cross-sectional data reveal that race is an important correlate in personal crimes, with the magnitude of the sex effect larger than the race effect, but each effect is very pronounced (Hindelang, 1978, 1981).

Although not receiving as much research attention as female offenders, the issue of changes in offending by racial subgroups is of

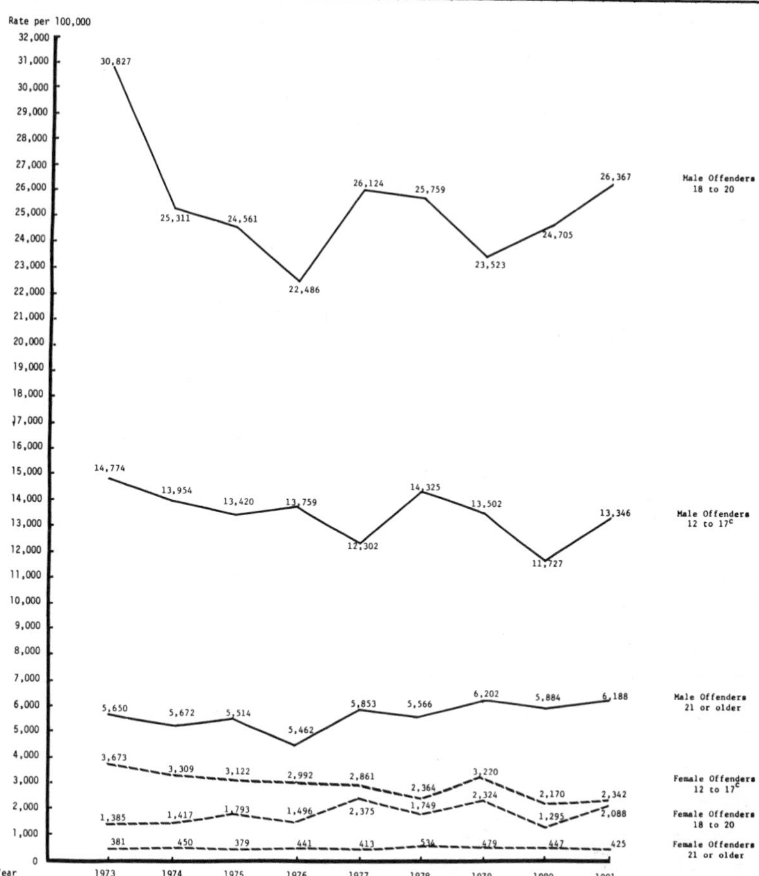

a. Includes perceived age of lone and perceived age of oldest multiple offender.
b. Excluded are incidents (about 10% of the total) in which the victim did not know whether there was one or more than one offender and incidents involving offenders of "mixed" sexes.
c. The numerator of the rates of offending for 12- to 17-year-olds excludes incidents (about 1% of the total) in which the offender was perceived by the victim to be under 12 years of age. The denominator of the rate is the number of 12- to 17-year-olds in the general population.

Figure 4.1 Estimated Annual Rates of Offending in Total Personal Crimes (per 100,000 potential offenders in each population subgroup) by Year, Age of Offender,[a] and Sex of Offender, NCS National Data, 1973-1981[b]

equal concern and controversy. Explicit attention on the serious violent juvenile is often implicit concern about black juvenile offenders. It is important then to examine the yearly NCS data to determine whether or

TABLE 4.2 Estimated Rates of Offending (per 100,000 potential offenders in each population subgroup), by Age of Offender,[a] Race of Offender, and Type of Crime, NCS National Data, 1973-1981 Aggregate[b]

Age and Race of Offender	*Type of Crime*					
	Rape	*Robbery*	*Aggravated Assault*	*Simple Assault*	*Personal Larceny*	*Total Personal Crimes*
12 to 17[c]						
White	50	784	1,215	3,281	147	5,477
Black	346	8,455	4,432	9,714	2,249	25,196
18 to 20						
White	136	1,337	2,708	4,810	197	9,188
Black	567	17,056	7,682	10,670	3,733	39,473
21 or older						
White	70	277	696	1,161	47	2,252
Black	337	3,368	2,273	2,824	691	9,494

a. Includes perceived age of lone and perceived age of oldest multiple offender.
b. Excluded are incidents (about 8% of the total) in which the victim did not know whether there was one or more than one offender and incidents involving offenders of other and "mixed" races.
c. The numerator of the rates of offending for 12- to 17-year-olds excludes incidents (about 1% of the total) in which the offender was perceived by the victim to be under 12 years of age. The denominator of the rate is the number of 12- to 17-year-olds in the general population.

not there have been changes in the rate of offending across racial subgroups.

Figure 4.2 displays rates of offending in total personal crimes by age and race of offender for the 1973-1981 period. The large differences between the black and white offending rates found in the cross-sectional data are consistently revealed in the trend data. These data also reveal that while white juvenile offenders register virtually no change in their rate of offending, black juveniles show an overall declining trend (37%) in their rate of offending for this period. Note though in Figure 4.2 that the trend line for black juvenile offenders displays an upturn in 1981. The 1981 data notwithstanding, it appears that the 1973 to 1981 decline in juvenile offending is attributable in part to the decline in rates of offending in total personal crimes among black juveniles.

AGE, RACE, AND SEX OF OFFENDER

Questions relating to age, race, sex, and criminal behavior are as inherently complex as they are interesting. Typically, researchers have focused on one key variable, say sex, without considering interaction effects with other important variables. In part this is due to the fact that most researchers have relied on Uniform Crime Report (UCR) data and within published UCR data no tables are available by age, race, and sex of arrestees simultaneously. Unfortunately, alternative data sources such as national self-reports of offending behavior in the general population (Elliott et al., 1981) have been of limited utility in shedding light on issues relating to the age, race, and sex of offenders because of inadequate sample size.

The data in Table 4.3 present the simultaneous effects of sex, race, and age subgroups for the 1973-1981 period as a whole. Generally, in the 12 to 17, 18 to 20, and 21 or older age groups, black males have the highest rate of offending, white males the second highest rate, black females the third highest, and white females the lowest rate of offending. Among female offenders, there is a decline in the rates of offending in personal crimes as age increases; black females in each age group generally are about three to five times as likely as their white counterparts to offend in face-to-face personal crimes. When the data are examined among males, the black to white offending rate ratio is also about 4 to 5:1. Among males, the curvilinear pattern by age evident above is also apparent here.

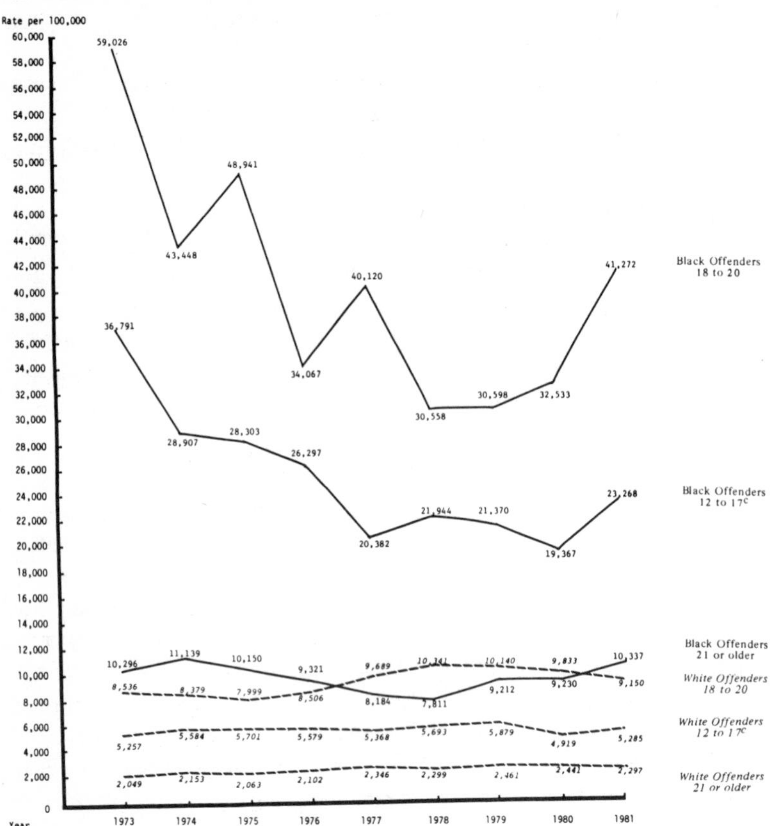

a. Includes perceived age of lone and perceived age of oldest multiple offender.
b. Excluded are incidents (about 8% of the total) in which the victim did not know whether there was one or more than one offender and incidents involving offenders of "mixed" race.
c. The numerator of the rates of offending for 12- to 17-year-olds excludes incidents (about 1% of the total) in which the offender was perceived by the victim to be under 12 years of age. The denominator of the rate is the number of 12- to 17-year-olds in the general population.

Figure 4.2 Estimated Annual Rates of Offending in Total Personal Crimes (per 100,000 potential offenders in each population subgroup) by Year, Age of Offender,[a] and Race of Offender, NCS National Data, 1973-1981[b]

Similar aggregate patterns of offending are also evident when crime-specific rates of offending are analyzed by age, race, and sex of offender. Again, the trends in NCS data are consistent with aggregate patterns.

TABLE 4.3 Estimated Rates of Offending (per 100,000 potential offenders in each population subgroup), by Age of Offender,[a] Race of Offender, Sex of Offender, and Type of Crime, NCS National Data, 1973-1981 Aggregate[b]

Age, Race, and Sex of Offender	*Type of Crime*					*Total Personal Crimes*
	Rape	*Robbery*	*Aggravated Assault*	*Simple Assault*	*Personal Larceny*	
12 to 17[c]						
White males	89	1,259	2,051	4,280	234	7,914
Black males	586	15,240	6,369	12,704	3,930	38,829
White females	–	166	206	1,598	35	2,012
Black females	–	903	1,258	4,344	389	6,946
18 to 20						
White males	271	2,345	4,867	8,159	349	15,992
Black males	1,193	33,905	14,025	18,338	6,763	74,223
White females	–	80	255	841	34	1,213
Black females	–	849	1,063	1,756	798	4,487
21 or older						
White males	142	504	1,232	2,016	70	3,964
Black males	737	6,862	3,821	5,122	1,175	17,716
White females	–	31	71	182	16	301
Black females	–	179	470	573	177	1,402

a. Includes perceived age of lone and perceived age of oldest multiple offender.

b. Excluded are incidents (about 11% of the total) in which the victim did not know whether there was one or more than one offender and incidents involving offenders of "mixed" sexes or races.

c. The numerator of the rates of offending for 12- to 17-year-olds excludes incidents (about 1% of the total) in which the offender was perceived by the victim to be under 12 years of age. The denominator of the rate is the number of 12- to 17-year-olds in the general population.

DATA LIMITATIONS

The general limitations of NCS data have been extensively reviewed elsewhere (see Hindelang, 1976; Hindelang et al., 1978; Penick and Owens, 1976). These problems include the limited number of crime types that are available for analysis compared with UCR and self-report data; the problems of underreporting nonstranger victimizations to survey interviewers; and, finally, the potential for aggregation bias when examining national-level data.

Moreover, there are four interrelated limitations regarding the use of NCS data in connection with studying offender characteristics. First, because the source of the data is the victim's report, only a small number of visible offender characteristics are available—sex, race, age, and number of offenders, and relationship to the victim. For example, no information is available on the socioeconomic status of offenders. Second, little systematic work had been done on the accuracy of the victim's reports of these offender variables (see Laub, 1983a, for a review). Third, because these data depend on reports of victims, they include only offenses in which the victim sees the offender: rape, robbery, assault, and personal larceny with contact between the victim and offender. Fourth, questions related to incidence versus prevalence cannot be resolved with these data. For example, the question of whether the disproportionate number of males among offenders is due to a small proportion of males repeatedly offending or due to a large proportion of males rarely offending cannot be resolved with these data (Hindelang and McDermott, 1981).

CONCLUSION

One advantage of using social indicator data, such as the National Crime Survey or the Uniform Crime Reports, is that these large-scale data sets allow researchers to identify the correlates of offending. Of course, if different data sets agree as to the basic correlates of offending, overall confidence in the findings is increased and these results can become useful for purposes of theory development and theory testing.

The ability of the NCS data to identify the high-rate offending subgroups among the available demographic characteristics is clear. Despite the data limitations noted above, the magnitude of the differences are strong and unlikely to be altered significantly due to biases in the NCS data. Moreover, substantial agreement across official and self-report data sets exists regarding the age and sex of offenders.

Yet even if these large-scale data sets were in total agreement as to the correlates question, the implications for criminological theory would not be straightforward. In part, this is due to the problem that Kornhauser (1978: 82, emphasis in original) noted,

> Most delinquency theories take as their point of departure the *same* "independent variables." Age, sex, race, ethnicity, socioeconomic status, size of community—these are the staples of delinquency theory. Even if securely established, the correlation of any or all of these with delinquency is compatible with all extant theories.

Kornhauser goes on to say that our focus ought to be on the "intervening variables" between demographic correlates and delinquency/crime.

In order to facilitate this etiological research, we need to merge our analyses of social indicator data (UCR, NCS) with special in-depth studies of individual subgroups. One method that could be adapted for this purpose is oral histories of offenders and victims (Laub, 1984). Through skillful, detailed interviews, insights can be acquired into the dynamics of offending and victimization. For instance, we now know very little about the interrelationship of offending and victimization. The oral history method can open up such new areas of investigation. As Plummer (1983: 72) notes, "In areas of inquiry about which little is known, the life history technique can become a sensitizing tool to the kinds of issues and problems involved in that field. It is especially useful in areas in which conceptualization of problems has been ill worked out." Oral histories are then particularly helpful in identifying new variables for study and analysis.

Oral histories would also enhance our ability to sort out the interaction of key variables such as age, race, sex, and social class and provide specification and meaning of these variables. Kobrin (1982: 163) argues essentially this point.

> Even the conditions associated with, for example, social class, ethnicity, age, gender, and similar descriptors of social locations are themselves variables as, at the level of behavior, their meanings are taken into account by the actor in his development of a stable pattern of action. The problem thus becomes that of discerning the regularities in the ways persons of defined categories perceive the meanings they attribute to elements of social location.

Oral histories can provide valuable insights into such complexities.

Finally, and perhaps most important, oral histories permit the researcher to study the social process—the ordering of events over time, the duration of events, the intensity of events, and so on. Although there is growing concern with juvenile crime, we have little data on the behavior of juveniles in general. For instance, how do juveniles spend their time? In a given day, how much time is spent with peers? parents? at school? work? Examination of such questions can shed light on the processes of offending and victimization as well as the processing of sanctioning illegal or deviant behaviors. Oral histories are well-suited for such an analysis.

While large-scale data sets such as the National Crime Survey victimization data provide a more than adequate foundation for a positivist criminology, these existing data need to be supplemented by more in-depth analyses of individual subgroups in the population. One promising avenue of data collection is the oral history method. With such tools, positivist criminology can continue to make substantial contributions.

5

Social Class and Crime

JOSEPH G. WEIS

More research and theoretical attention has been devoted to the role of social class in the etiology of crime than to any other variable. The empirical relation between social class and criminal behavior was first established with ecological correlations and official crime data (Shaw and McKay, 1942), while the theoretical relation has been made a central etiological dynamic in most major theories of crime, including strain (Cloward and Ohlin, 1960), conflict (Quinney, 1977), cultural deviance (Miller, 1958), and labeling (Schur, 1971) perspectives. With the notable exception of control theory (Hirschi, 1969), contemporary theories of crime depend on a robust, significant, and meaningful negative correlation between social class and crime. According to some scholars, this relationship is a "thoroughly documented" fact (Gordon, 1976: 201); to others its documentation as a predominant correlate is inconsistent, weak, and unconvincing (Hindelang et al., 1981).

There are two critical research issues regarding the apparently elusive correlation between social class and crime. The first was raised by the startling finding of no relationship between self-reported delinquent behavior and parents' socioeconomic status (Short and Nye, 1958). The second issue was raised by recent work on the measurement of crime, particularly on the discrepancy between correlations produced by different measurement methods (Hindelang et al., 1979). If there is a negative correlation between social class and crime, is it found in both official and self-report measures of crime? Discrepant correlations may reflect empirical reality or inadequate measurement.

The controversy surrounding these research issues continues, but most research is incapable of assessing them because studies typically rely on only one measure of crime, either official data or self-reports, precluding a direct comparison of the correlations generated by each measurement method on the same sample. Usually it is assumed that there is a strong inverse relation between class and official crime and the self-report estimates are compared with this standard. However, this relationship was established with ecological correlations that tend to overestimate substantially individual-level correlations (Robinson, 1959; Hannan 1971). And it is not clear that there is, indeed, a relationship between social class and official measures of crime.

Two meta-analyses of the class-crime relationship come to opposite conclusions regarding the correlation between social class and official crime measures. Tittle et al. (1978) report no important relationship, while Braithwaite (1981) concludes in a later review that there is some evidence to support an official crime-class correlation. Finally, when one examines those studies using individual-level official data only (Hathaway and Monachesi, 1963; Havighurst, 1962; Polk et al., 1974), the relationship between social class and official delinquency is weakly negative to nonexistent (Hindelang et al., 1981: 187-188). A more recent longitudinal study of a cohort of 7,719 boys in Stockholm (Janson, 1982) also reports no important individual-level relationship between a family's social position and a boy having a police record.

Self-report studies typically also report no relationship between individual-level measures of self-reported crime and class (e.g., Akers, 1964: Dentler and Monroe, 1961; Gold, 1970; Hindelang, 1973; Bachman et al., 1978). However, there is a recent exception to the trend in reported findings of self-report studies. Elliott and Ageton (1980) report from analyses of the National Youth Survey (NYS) probability sample of approximately 1,500 youths that there is a moderate inverse relationship between socioeconomic status and serious "person crimes" and serious "property crimes," particularly for the former among black youths. Later analyses of the panel for 1976 to 1980 show small to moderate class differences in prevalence and incidence for serious crimes, and the relationship is stronger for incidence than prevalence scales (Elliott and Huizinga, 1983).

The small number of studies that are capable of assessing rigorously the discrepancy between social class and official and self-report measures of crime show somewhat mixed results. Of the five major studies reviewed by Hindelang, Hirschi, and Weis (1981: 188-193) that have *both* individual-level official and self-report measures on the same sample, all showed convergent estimates of the correlation between social class *and* official and self-reported crime (Reiss and Rhodes, 1961; Williams and Gold, 1972; Elliott and Voss, 1974; Hirschi, 1969; Wolfgang et al., 1972). Four of these studies reported convergence around no relationship, while only one showed convergent estimates of a small inverse relationship (Reiss and Rhodes, 1961). (Official data have also been collected as part of the ongoing National Youth Survey [Elliott and Ageton, 1980; Elliott and Huizinga, 1983], but they have not been reported in the literature in a direct assessment of discrepancy. One can only speculate that this analysis will show convergence around an inverse relationship, since one is being reported between social class and self-reported crime.) One other study, based on the Cambridge Study in Delinquent Development, finds a lagged inverse relationship between social class at age fourteen and conviction at seventeen through twenty but not to self-reported crime at age eighteen (Farrington, 1982: 17; 1979). However, this unusual discrepancy is only one among a much broader pattern in the study of no important differences between self-report and official record estimates of a variety of correlates.

Two other major studies report convergent correlations. In an important reanalysis of the follow-up interview data from the Philadelphia cohort study, Thornberry and Farnworth (1982) report that there is no important relationship between status, as measured primarily by educational attainment, and criminal involvement, whether measured by self-report interview or official police arrest data, when the cohort members were *juveniles*. However, there was a significant inverse relationship between status and both official and self-reported crime when the cohort members were *adults*. That is, convergent estimates of the class-crime relationship are produced for juveniles and adults, but they are in different directions. Apparently, the effect of social class varies by age status—one should not assume that the operation of social class is the same at fifteen as it is at twenty-five.

Finally, Hindelang et al. (1979) propose that the alleged discrepancy between self-report and official measures for social class, as well as for gender and race, becomes "illusory" when standard but critical methodological considerations are taken into account, particularly comparisons of results by level of measurement and by the domain, content, and seriousness of criminal behavior. If the data are properly analyzed by comparing individual-level measures of both official and self-reported crime with individual-level measures of class, *and* the types and seriousness of crimes compared are the same, the alleged discrepancy for social class is resolved. A comprehensive empirical test of these hypotheses shows that there is a very weak, insignificant relationship with socioeconomic status when one controls for level of measurement and compares individual-level data on both variables. It seems that no matter how one measures, scores, or scales the data there are small, typically negative relations between social class and juvenile crime, whether official or self-report. The correlations (gamma) range from –.01 to –.08 between occupation of principal wage earner and the self-reported delinquency prevalence scales (Total, Serious Crime, General Delinquency, Drug Use, Family-School Offenses) and the total official offenses index (Hindelang, Hirschi, and Weis, 1981: 181-198). In short, there is not the kind of robust relationship between social class and either self-reported or official juvenile crime that most contemporary theories of crime propose should exist.

THE CURRENT STUDY

These results are perplexing because a few rigorous studies report a moderate inverse relation between social class and self-reported crime (e.g., Elliott and Ageton, 1980; Elliott and Huizinga, 1983), while more equally rigorous studies show an absent to weak inverse relation for *both* self-report and official measures (e.g., Hindelang, Hirschi, and Weis, 1981; Thornberry and Farnworth, 1982). In an effort to clarify the current confusion, analyses of the social class and juvenile crime relationship in the Seattle Youth Study (SYS) data set will be carried further than reported in Hindelang, Hirschi, and Weis (1981). The continuing search for the elusive correlation between social class and crime will focus on methodological and substantive factors that might produce a meaningful correlation.

First, given the apparent success in finding an inverse relationship between class and delinquency in the NYS, the procedures used by Elliott and Ageton (1980) and Elliott and Huizinga (1983) will be replicated as closely as possible. In addition to the same methodological adjustments (same level of measurement, domain, content, and seriousness of offenses) recommended by Hindelang et al. (1979), they offer the additional suggestions that the proper analysis of self-report data should include more attention to scoring and scaling of items. Specifically, Elliott et al. argue that the reported frequency of illegal acts should not be restricted in the scoring of individuals and that the unique properties and contributions of individual crimes that may be related to social class (or other variables) not be masked or lost in global scales of delinquency. (Elliott and Ageton [1980] and Elliott and Huizinga [1983] report an inverse relationship between social class and self-reported delinquency based on these suggested methodological adjustments. They also propose, as one would expect, that it is the "methodological inadequacy" of the self-report method that is probably the source of the discrepancy between the results of self-report and official measures. However, in neither of these papers do they report any official data on their sample or, therefore, any comparisons of correlates that would allow one to assess directly the issue of discrepancy in the NYS sample.)

Accordingly, these analyses will also use unrestricted incidence rather than prevalence scores of criminal involvement during the past year; NYS scales will be replicated in scale analyses; item analyses will be performed, particularly for those crimes that are included in the NYS scales; and the analytic procedures and statistics utilized in Elliott and Ageton (1980) and Elliott and Huizinga (1983) will be employed in the current analyses. Perhaps these additional methodological refinements will generate correlations in the SYS similar to those discovered in the NYS.

Second, if replicating the technical tinkering with the self-report measurement method does not also replicate the elusive inverse correlation, one of a number of substantive factors—particularly potential "ecological context" effects—will be explored that may help specify the relation between social class and crime.

The data to be analyzed were collected during the 1978-1979 academic year in Seattle, Washington on a random sample of over 1,600 youths, stratified by sex, race (black, white), socioeconomic status (high, low), and delinquency status (nondelinquent, police record, court record). Both official records of police and court contact and self-reports of involvement in 69 "chargeable offenses" were collected on the sample, as well as other demographic and social information. Males, blacks, lower SES, and official delinquents were oversampled in order to facilitate analysis on those variables of etiological and methodological interest that are often under-represented in general random or probability samples. The data were collected within a quasi-experimental design to assess the effects of different measurement methods on estimates of the prevalence, incidence, and, particularly, correlates of juvenile crime. (See Hindelang, Hirschi, and Weis, 1981: 27-41 for a complete description of the research design, sample, and data.)

In order to replicate the procedures used in the analysis of the NYS, one social-class scale and two sets of self-reported delinquency scales were simulated with the SYS data. Following Elliott and Ageton (1980), a set of *offense-category* scales was constructed, and following Elliott and Huizinga (1983), a set of *offense-specific* scales was constructed (Table 5.1). In total, 37 of the 69 self-report items in the Seattle data are included in these various scales; they also serve as the basis of the item-by-item analyses. The scales are past year *incidence* scales, computed by adding frequency responses to questions "How many times in the past year have you . . . ?" The incidence reported for an item is not restricted or truncated in any meaningful way—the reported frequency of involvement for a crime may range from 0-998. There were only a few items for a few respondents with higher frequencies, and the variance with the given range should be sufficient to show a relationship if it exists.

The three social class categories used in the analyses of the NYS were simulated by converting the SYS occupational and educational codes into their equivalents in the Hollingshead Two Factor Index of Social Position (Miller, 1977: 230-238). Following the Hollingshead scoring procedures, as did Elliott and Ageton (1980) and Elliott and Huizinga (1983), a social position score was computed for each member of the sample, who was then assigned to the corresponding middle-, working-, or lower-class category. Apparently, social class has been trichotomized in order to facilitate comparisons based on group means and differences (e.g., ANOVA, t-test), rather than those based on individual attributes and difference (e.g., correlation).

Using these simulated scales, the original SYS scales, and individual delinquency items, the analyses reported here will attempt to discover and specify, once again, the relation between social class and juvenile crime.

ECOLOGICAL MEASURES OF CLASS

As reported by Hindelang, Hirschi, and Weis (1981: 194, 196), ecological measures of social class do not show even a moderate relation with either self-report or official measures of juvenile crime. The largest gamma (–.17) is between official delinquency and social status as measured by median income of the census tract in which respondents live. The relations with the self-reported delinquency prevalence scales (Total, Serious Crime, General Delinquency, Drug Use, Family-School Offenses) are even smaller, ranging from .01 to –.06. When additional ecological measures of social class (percentage of families below the poverty level; percentage of residents below the poverty level; percentage

TABLE 5.1 Comparison of Self-Reported Delinquency Scale Items

National Youth Survey (NYS)	*Seattle Youth Study (SYS)*
Offense–Specific	
Felony Assault	
Aggravated assault	Seriously injure victim
Sexual assault	Forced sex
Gang fights	Jumped and beat up someone
Minor Assault	
Hit teacher	Hit teacher
Hit parents	Hit parents
Hit students	Picked fight with stranger
Robbery	
Strongarmed students	Robbery with weapon
Strongarmed teachers	Strongarm robbery
Strongarmed others	
Felony Theft	
Bought stolen goods	Bought stolen goods
Stole something greater than $50	Shoplift greater than $50
Stole motor vehicle	Broke into car
Broke into buildings/vehicle	Burglary
	Breaking and entering
Minor Theft	
Joyriding	Took car
Stole something less than $5	Shoplifting less than $2
Stole something $5-50	Shoplifting $10-50
Damaged Property	
Damaged family property	Broke up furniture
Damaged school property	Broke school windows
Damaged other property	Broke car windows
	Broke windows/empty building
	Slash seats
	Destroy mailboxes
	Destruction at construction site
Drug Use	(Hard Drug Use)
Hallucinogens	LSD, PCP, Mescaline
Barbiturates	Barbiturates
Heroin	Heroin
Cocaine	Cocaine
Amphetamines	
Offense–Category	
Illegal Services	(Selling Drugs)
Sold hard drugs	Sold illegal drugs
Sold marijuana	
Prostitution	

Continued

TABLE 5.1 Continued

National Youth Survey (NYS)	*Seattle Youth Study (SYS)*
Public Disorder	(Disorderly Conduct)
Hitchhiked illegally	Carried weapon
Disorderly conduct	Smoked marijuana
Public drunkenness	High/drunk at school
Panhandled	
Obscene calls	
Status Offenses	
Runaway	Runaway
Skipped classes	Cut school
Lied about age	Drank beer/wine
Sexual intercourse	Drank hard liquor
Person Crimes	
Aggravated assault	Seriously injured victim
Gang fights	Jumped and beat up victim
Hit teacher	Hit teacher
Hit parent	Hit parent
Hit students	Picked fight with stranger
Sexual assault	Forced sex
Strongarmed students	Robbery with weapon
Strongarmed teachers	Strongarm robbery
Strongarmed others	
General Theft	(Property Crimes)
Stole something greater than $50	Shoplifted greater than $50
Stole something less than $5	Shoplifted less than $2
Stole something $5-50	Shoplifted $10-50
Bought stolen goods	Bought stolen goods
Joyriding	Took car
Stole motor vehicle	Broke into car
Broke into buildings/vehicle	Breaking and entering
	Burglary
	Sell stolen goods
	Stole from desk, locker
	Broke car windows
	Broke school windows
	Broke windows, empty building
	Broke up furniture
	Slashed seats
	Destroyed mailboxes
	Destruction at construction site

of labor force "middle class" or in managerial and professional occupations; percentage of families receiving welfare; median income of families) are examined for their relation with other delinquency scales—

the NYS self-report scales (Person, Property, Illegal Service, Public Disorder, Hard Drug Use, Status Offenses)—the relationship is virtually the same (Table 5.2). For example, the largest correlation (.07) is between property crimes and median family income. The strongest relation among whites is between total offenses and median family income (.06), whereas for blacks it is between person crimes and median family income (–.06). And the other four ecological measures show similar weak relations with these self-reported delinquency scales.

The relations with the three official measures of delinquency—Police Contacts Ever, Police Contacts Past Year, Juvenile Court Referrals Ever—also show weak but slightly larger coefficients. For example, the strongest relation for the total sample is between percentage families on welfare with police contacts ever (.10); the highest for whites (.07) and blacks (.12) are also with police contacts ever. Apparently, as the percentage of welfare families in a census tract increases, there is a weak relationship with police contacts.

Overall, these additional analyses of the relation between a variety of ecological measures of class and a variety of self-report and official measures of juvenile crime, confirm Hindelang, Hirschi, and Weis (1981). But, the data suggest that there may be ecological factors that affect the social class-official delinquency relation. This may be associated with the ecological contexts within which different types of youths reside—this possibility will be explored later.

INDIVIDUAL MEASURES OF CLASS

At the individual level of measurement of both social class and self-reported and official delinquency, there are, again, uniformly small and typically negative correlations that range from –.01 to –.08 between occupation of principal wage earner and the SYS self-report and official delinquency scales (Hindelang, Hirschi, and Weis, 1981: 196). When one goes beyond these analyses and (a) uses the same SYS plus the NYS self-report scales but scored for incidence or the total unrestricted frequency within the past year; (b) examines each of the three official delinquency indexes (Police Contacts Ever, Police Contacts Past Year, Juvenile Court Referrals Ever); (c) does an item-by-item analysis of the self-reported delinquency items; and (d) examines each of their (a, b, c) relationships with social class separately with a variety of indicators of socioeconomic status, including father's education, father's occupation, mother's education, mother's occupation, father employed, mother

TABLE 5.2 Self-Reported Delinquency Scales by Ecological Measures of Class: National Youth Survey Scales, Census Tract-Level Measures of Class, Pearson Correlations

	Middle Class[a]	*Median Family Income*	*Families Below Poverty*	*Residents Below Poverty*	*Families Receiving Welfare*	*Black*
Total SRD	.04	.06*	–.02	–.02	–.01	–.04
Person crimes	.01	.01	.01	.02	.00	.02
Property crimes	.02	.07*	–.04	–.04	.01	–.04
Selling drugs	.02	.03	–.02	–.02	–.01	–.02
Disorderly conduct	.03	.04	.00	–.01	.01	–.01
Hard drug use	.01	.00	–.01	.00	.00	–.02
Status offenses	.05*	.04	–.02	–.01	–.02	–.05*

a. Middle class refers to percentage employed in managerial or professional occupations.
*$p \leqslant .05$.

employed, father's socioeconomic status, and mother's socioeconomic status, one *still* finds consistenly weak to nonexistent relations that at times are in the wrong direction.

Beginning with the SYS self-reported delinquency scales, the strongest relation is –.09 between family-school offenses and father's education. The relations between the NYS scales and the eight individual-level measures of class are also consistently weak and negative, ranging from .04 to –.07 (Table 5.3). For the three SYS official delinquency indexes, the relations are similarly weak. The strongest relation (–.08) is between juvenile court referrals ever and father's education (Table 5.4). Finally, an item-by-item analysis of the 69 self-reported criminal acts also produces consistently weak correlations with each indicator of social class. The strongest relation for the total sample is –.08 for skipping school and mother's education; among whites the largest correlation is –.09 between skipping school and mother's education, while for blacks it is .17 between purse/wallet theft and mother's socioeconomic status. (A natural log transformation of all of the self-reported delinquency items and scales was performed in order to linearize the distribution, and the same analysis was run with the same results. This standardization procedure, though different from Z scores, typically creates bigger associations between self-reported delinquency and other variables in correlational analysis. Here it did not make much difference.)

Overall, these findings from correlational analyses further substantiate a systematically weak relationship between a variety of measures of social class and (1) a variety of self-reported delinquency incidence scales, (2) a variety of official crime indexes, and (3) a number of self-report items, all at the individual level of measurement. These findings also provide more evidence that there is no discrepancy in the correlation between social class and official or self-report measures of crime.

Given that Elliott and Ageton (1980) were able to tease out an inverse relation between social class and predatory person crimes, especially among blacks, by analyzing group differences in juvenile crime, it may be possible to discover similar relations in the SYS data by replicating their procedures.

ANALYSIS OF SOCIAL CLASS GROUP DIFFERENCES

Analyses of variance on the relationship between the NYS self-reported delinquency scales and tripartite social class categories,

TABLE 5.3 Self-Reported Delinquency Scales by Individual-Level Measures of Class: National Youth Survey Scales, Individual-Level Measures of Class, Pearson Correlations

	Father's Education	*Father's Occupation*	*Father's Employment*	*Father's SES*	*Mother's Education*	*Mother's Occupation*	*Mother's Employment*	*Mother's SES*
Total SRD	–.07*	.04	–.07*	–.02	–.03	–.03	–.06*	–.02
Person crimes	–.01	–.02	.00	–.05*	–.01	.00	–.02	.00
Property crimes	–.04	.02	–.04	–.01	–.06*	.02	.01	.02
Selling drugs	–.02	–.02	.00	.01	–.01	–.01	.02	–.02
Disorderly conduct	–.07*	.03	–.07*	–.02	–.01	–.03	–.07*	–.03
Hard drug use	–.02	.00	–.01	.00	.00	.01	–.02	.01
Status offenses	–.02	.02	–.05*	.01	–.02	–.03	–.04	.00

*$p \leq .05$.

TABLE 5.4 Official Delinquency by Individual-Level Measures of Class: Seattle Youth Study Indexes, Individual-Level Measures of Class, Pearson Correlations

	Father's Education	*Father's Occupation*	*Father's SES*	*Mother's Education*	*Mother's Occupation*	*Mother's SES*
Police contacts, ever	–.06*	–.06*	.07*	–.07*	–.06*	–.07*
Police contacts, past year	–.02	–.04	–.04	-.04	–.05*	–.05
Juvenile court referrals, ever	–.08*	–.06*	–.07*	–.06*	–.04	–.04

*$p \leqslant .05$.

support the findings of the prior correlational analyses. Using mean standardized scores on the offense-category scales and class divisions based on father's socioeconomic status, there are no significant or meaningful relationships between social class and self-reported delinquency (Table 5.5).

The SYS data once again allow similar analyses of variance on the relation between class and official delinquency. Here there is one significant relation ($f = 3.115$; $p = .05$) between police contacts ever and father's occupation among the many differences compared. This is a significant but small correlation, which may reflect the large size of the total sample. This artifactual quality is supported by the absence of significant relations between official delinquency and social class among whites and blacks. And analyses of variance show that there are no statistically significant relations between self-reported delinquency and class among the official delinquents in the sample who have police and juvenile court records. It seems that even among the "most delinquent" members of the sample there is a consistently weak correlation. Given the hundreds of differences computed, it is difficult to know if this is a meaningful or "chance" significant difference. It is definitely not part of a consistent pattern of inverse relationships between social class and crime.

Following Elliott and Huizinga (1983), social-class group differences on offense-category scales, offense-specific scales, and individual delinquency items were analyzed using pooled variance t-tests. (The assumptions underlying this type of t-test are less conservative than those in the tests used by Elliott and Huizinga [1983]. That is, the t-tests used here are more likely to show a relation, so if one exists, it is even more likely to emerge in these analyses.) The comparisons were performed for the entire sample, white males, and black males. For the entire sample and black males, there are no significant differences among any of the three social-class groups on all of the self-reported offense-category and offense-specific scales. Among white males, there are no significant differences on any of the offense-category scales, but there is one significant difference between the middle and lower class on one of the offense-specific scales—damaged property. Here, the lower-class boys are more involved than middle-class boys in damaging property. Overall, this means that there is one significant difference among the 108 comparisons of the twelve self-reported delinquency scales by the three social-class categories for the three groups of respondents. This could be a random significant finding.

TABLE 5.5 Self-Reported Delinquency Scales by Father's SES: National Youth Survey Scales and SES Categories, Mean Standardized Scale Scores, One-Way Analysis of Variance

Class	N	$\overline{X}$	SD	N	$\overline{X}$	SD	N	$\overline{X}$	SD	N	$\overline{X}$	SD
	Total SRD			*Person Crimes*			*Property Crimes*			*Selling Drugs*		
Lower	383	−.130	12.118	444	.218	4.473	417	.204	8.058	452	.008	1.019
Working	253	−.151	14.996	299	−.018	4.618	283	.064	7.067	303	.014	1.044
Middle	277	−.213	11.243	304	−.194	2.736	292	−.369	4.500	306	.100	1.482
F	.004			.560			.557			.210		
p ⩽	.996			.571			.573			.811		
	Disorderly Conduct			*Hard Drug Use*			*Status Offenses*					
Lower	432	−.129	1.706	450	.036	3.116	422	−.032	2.387			
Working	290	.032	2.337	311	−.179	.766	297	−.058	2.584			
Middle	307	.050	2.274	314	.104	3.650	307	.182	3.151			
F	.891			1.224			1.686					
p ⩽	.410			.295			.186					

The results of the item analysis are more mixed. For the entire sample, there are six significant differences in the expected direction between the social-class groups on four crimes—robbery with a weapon, jumped and beat someone up, shoplifting greater than $50, and breaking windows in an empty building (Table 5.6). These four crimes are among the most serious of the 37 self-reported offenses tested. They involve violent crimes against the person and high-value crimes against property. And the largest number of significant differences (four) on these crimes are between middle- and lower-class youths, findings similar to those reported by Elliott and Ageton (1980) and Elliott and Huizinga (1983). (A seventh significant difference shows middle-class youths more frequently drunk or high at school than lower-class youths, t = 2.17; significance = .03.

These results must be placed within the appropriate analytic context—the six statistically significant differences represent less than 5% of all 111 comparisons made and each has a small t-value (ranging around 2.0) that is just above the cut-off point for significance given the sample size. Additionally, the same tests performed separately for white males and black males provide a broader perspective on these findings. Among the white males, there are also six significant differences in the expected direction. Lower-class boys are more involved than middle-class boys in robbery with a weapon, shoplifting greater than $50, breaking windows in an empty building, and the use of hard drugs. Lower-class boys are more involved than working-class boys in taking a car and breaking windows in an empty building. Among the black males, there is only one significant difference between middle- and lower-class boys on breaking windows in an empty building.

Again, the differences between middle- and lower-class youths are most prominent, and for the more serious crimes, as one would expect. However, these additional comparisons contribute to a total of only 13 significant social-class differences among 333 comparisons—representing less than 4% of the total and, perhaps, random differences. However, the apparently more regular middle- versus lower-class differences on similar serious crimes suggest that the differences are not random, particularly for the entire sample and white males. But the almost virtual absence of class differences among black males supports the overall perception of a weak, unsystematic class effect.

If social class affects involvement in only a small number of certain types of crime among only certain types of offenders (and it is not clear from the data that this is so), the evidence from these analyses of

TABLE 5.6 Self-Reported Delinquent Acts by Social Class: National Youth Survey SES Categories, Significant Differences Only,[a] Pooled Variance T-Tests

Crime	*Class Group*	*N*	$\overline{X}$	*SD*	*t-value*	*d.f.*	*2-Tailed Sig.*
Robbery, weapon	middle	344	.0116	.132	−2.24	737	.03
	working	395	.1038	.752			
Robbery, weapon	middle	344	.0166	.132	−2.04	832	.04
	lower	490	.1490	1.242			
Jump and beat up	middle	340	.0853	.511	−2.27	827	.02
	lower	489	.2597	1.352			
Shoplift more than $50	middle	343	.0146	.142	−2.23	831	.03
	lower	490	.1163	.837			
Break windows, empty building	middle	339	.2950	1.227	−2.22	822	.03
	lower	485	1.4103	9.205			
Break windows, empty building	working	391	.3913	2.117	−2.14	874	.03
	lower	485	1.4103	9.205			

a. Group differences were compared on 37 crimes; all other 105 comparisons were nonsignificant, except for one that was significant in the wrong direction.

social-class group differences lends support to the conclusion of the correctional analysis that there is no meaningful relationship between social class and crime. Most theories of crime and their validation research require a stronger, more systematic, and perhaps more pervasive class effect. In short, social class should be doing more etiological work than the evidence shows.

ECOLOGICAL CONTEXT EFFECTS: CENSUS TRACTS AND NEIGHBORHOODS

It is somewhat disturbing that the agreed upon standard methodological adjustments that need to be applied to these data comparisons (same level of measurement, same domain of criminal acts, more sensitive scoring and scaling procedures) do not go far enough in generating a meaningful relationship between social class and crime. Even type of sample design does not seem to generate predictable relationships; for example, the two national probability samples of youth (Williams and Gold, 1972; Elliott and Ageton, 1980) generate different relationships between self-reported delinquency and class, and the earlier NYS data show convergence around no relationship (Hindelang et al., 1981: 189). More "substantive" adjustments may need to be considered. For example, the fact that some self-report studies report no relationship between social class and crime, while others do, suggests that social class may operate in different ways in different ecological contexts, whether social area, neighborhood, community, or city (Reiss and Rhodes, 1961; Johnstone, 1978; Clark and Wenninger, 1962; Gordon, 1967; Krohn et al., 1980).

Theoretically, ecological context should affect the relationship between social class and crime—it provides the social milieu within which the daily, direct effects of those social, economic, and educational factors and relationships that make up "social class" are experienced as one grows, lives, and works. Where and among whom one experiences these effects should make a difference, perhaps even in relationship to one's criminal behavior. To see if ecological context does affect the influence of social class, one needs to examine the individual-level class-crime relation *within* different ecological contexts—for example, within a variety of neighborhoods in a city. The SYS data are unique in that both self-report and official crime measures can be used in this type of analysis because both can be linked to census tract through the address of respondents.

Beginning with census tract ecological contexts, the results once again show inconsistent weak negative relations. By trichotomizing the census tracts (N = 120) on each of six ecological variables (percentage of families below the poverty level; percentage of residents below poverty level; median income of families; percentage of families receiving welfare; percentage black; employment rate), one can look at the relation between the NYS self-report scales and the eight social-class indicators within each type of census tract ecological context. For example, for those respondents who live in census tracts where there is a small percentage (0%-3%) of families below the poverty level (low-poverty census tracts), the strongest relation between class and self-reported delinquency is –.11, between disorderly conduct and mother's employment status. In the medium-poverty census tracts (4%-10% of families below poverty level), it is between disorderly conduct and father's socioeconomic status (–.08). In the high-poverty census tracts (11%-40% of families below poverty level), the largest correlation is –.12, between property crimes and mother's education. These correlations are certainly in the right direction, but they are weak and, perhaps most important here, there is really no difference by type of census tract ecological context. The same analyses were also done for each of the other five census tract characteristics with similar results.

"Census tract" is really too small an ecological context to have much social meaning or impact on the lives of its residents. "Neighborhood" may be a more powerful social context for generating, or at least reinforcing and maintaining, class effects on criminal behavior, as well as on other phenomena. Seattle has fourteen neighborhoods that are linked with its "Seven Hills" and other identifiable areas in the city, each with its own name and identity, which are well recognized and even institutionalized on the maps of the city's Office of Community Development. These fourteen neighborhoods were divided into three groups based on the median income of families within their constituent census tracts, and then *within* each neighborhood context (high, middle, low) the relations between both the seven NYS self-report scales and three SYS official delinquency indexes and the eight social-class indicators were examined.

For the total sample, nearly all correlations are not significant. The strongest relations with self-reported delinquency within the three types of neighborhoods, from high- to middle- to low-median income, are –.12, –.10, and –.14. The strongest relations with official delinquency are similar: –.07, –.11, and –.13. These findings basically replicate the earlier Hindelang et al. (1981) work, and the earlier analyses here—there is still a weak negative relation between social class and crime within high, middle, and low socioeconomic status neighborhoods, *and* there is still no discrepancy between the self-report and official correlates of social class. Of some interest are the apparently stronger relations between both parents' education and delinquency within the middle-income neighborhoods. The middle-class value of education may have, one might hypothesize, a more substantial effect than other indicators of social class in those neighborhoods and among those families where education is important to occupation and socialization of children. In short, different components of social class may affect crime in different ways in different ecological contexts.

CONCLUSION

Most theories of criminal behavior are constructed around the assumption of a strong negative correlation between social class and crime. However, the empirical evidence shows that there is not the kind of meaningful inverse relationship between social class and both official and self-report measures of crime that are required for their empirical validation. To the contrary, extended analyses of the SYS data show that there is a systematically weak relationship, no matter how one measures, scales, or scores the data. The replication of analytic procedures used by Elliott and Ageton (1980) and Elliott and Huizinga (1983) in their discovery of an inverse relationship in the NYS data—unrestricted incidence scales, item analysis, tests of group differences—did not produce the same results. Except for a small number of social-class group differences on a few self-report items, these findings support the general conclusion that there is a systematically weak relationship between social class, measured by a number of different indicators, and variety of self-reported delinquency incidence scales, a number of official crime indexes, and a large number of self-reported crime items, all at the individual level of measurement. The findings also provide more evidence for convergence, rather than discrepancy, in the correlation between social class and official and self-report measures of crime. Perhaps social class as a correlate of crime is not so elusive after all—it may simply not exist as proposed or assumed by criminological theorists and researchers.

6

Communities and Crime

ROBERT J. SAMPSON

The study of communities and crime is making a comeback these days, or so it seems. A perusal of recent issues of major sociological and criminological journals reveals an increasing stream of studies analyzing the effect of ecological characteristics on the aggregate crime rate (see, e.g., Messner, 1982, 1983a, 1983b; DeFronzo, 1983; Blau and Blau, 1982; Parker and Smith, 1979, Crutchfield et al., 1982; Rosenfeld, 1982, 1984; Jacobs, 1981; Williams, 1984; Carroll and Jackson, 1983; Byrne, 1984; Sampson, 1984a). This evidence of interest is perhaps not unexpected. The field of criminology has always enjoyed a strong ecological tradition in delinquency, dating back in this country at least to the seminal works of Shaw and McKay. Despite the tradition of the ecological approach, however, the recent surge of empirical studies appears unprecedented.

Arguably the most prominent of recent studies in the ecological mold is Blau and Blau (1982). Their study of metropolitan structure and violent crime has stimulated numerous papers and debates. Close examination of the Blaus's article provides a clue as to the popularity of ecological studies. According to Blau and Blau (1982), the ecological or "structural" approach to the study of crime offers a distinctively sociological focus; by contrast, the study of individual behavior is suggested to reify psychological reductionism. Apparently, the ecological approach offers us a macrosocial perspective, and promises to deliver key insights to the effects of social structure on crime.

A review of the literature on communities and crime find this and other claims of recent research to be wanting, and the empirical results ambiguous. Notwithstanding the volume of studies utilizing aggregate units of analysis, our knowledge of community effects on crime rests largely on conjecture. Unfortunately, then, our state of knowledge is little better than that provided by Shaw and McKay. In fact, it is hard to resist the temptation to posit that we have actually regressed in both theory and methods. Be that as it may, this chapter reviews ecological criminology and addresses the following key issues:

- the confounding of individual-level and community effects and resulting implications for structural inferences
- the lack of attention to intervening processes that mediate the effects of structural conditions
- the viability of a community-level social control theory

There are of course numerous issues in the ecology of crime, such as the controversy over aggregate units of analysis (e.g., cities or neighborhoods), data sources (e.g., victimization versus official data), the tenability of recursive models, the ad hoc nature of ecological measures, and the ecological fallacy. However, these issues have been covered in detail elsewhere, and hence it is unlikely that we will gain much by rehashing old concerns. It is my contention that the issues covered in this chapter are central to the literature on communities and crime, yet have not been dealt with in satisfactory fashion to date in the literature.

Although my review suggests a seemingly pessimistic assessment of ecological research, I will maintain that the ecological approach *is* promising, and indeed appears to be an essential area of future inquiry. To this end, the latter section of this chapter sketches a research agenda implied by recently emerging community social control theory. Thus rather than offer what Kornhauser (1978: 1380) terms a "counsel of despair" in overviewing ecological research, I hope to keep within the spirit of this volume and identify empirical hypotheses that a positive criminology is uniquely capable of testing.

INDIVIDUALS AND SOCIAL STRUCTURE

One reason the ecological approach has gained currency in recent years is the apparent sociological precision resulting from a focus on social structure rather than individual behavior. Not surprisingly, one of the foremost sociologists advocating a structural approach is Blau. Recently he has devoted much of his attention to the problem of crime (Blau and Blau, 1982; Blau, 1981). Blau (1981: 171) argues that violent crime may be used to illustrate a "structural orientation in macrosociological inquiry." According to Blau (1981: 171), two *different* questions can be raised about crime:

> why some people commit them while others do not; or why their rates are higher in some social situations than in others. The first question conceptualizes crime as behavior engaged in by individuals, which leads to a psychological investigation . . . the second question conceptualizes crime as more or less prevalent conflict in a social environment—for instance, a city—and thus as a characteristic of the pattern of social relations in a place. In this case, the units of analysis are not individuals but cities or other collectivities, which leads to a sociological investigation.

Blau's comments seem to imply that *only* a structural analysis using macrosocial units is proper sociological study. In fact, Blau (1981: 171, emphasis added) argues exactly this, stressing that a "sociological perspective *requires* that groups or larger collectivities, not individuals, be units of analysis." If true, it is no wonder that numerous researchers have embraced the ecological approach in attempts to address "macrosociological" theory (see, e.g., Rosenfeld, 1984; Blau and Blau, 1982; Liska et al., 1981). Even using ecological units is not enough, though. Blau (1981: 171) further argues that "a proper sociological analysis involves not only collective units but also some variables that pertain to distinctive properties of these units, not to aggregate properties of the individuals composing them." And what are these distinctive properties? Among others, Blau (1981: 171) notes that economic inequality and racial composition are attributes that cannot characterize individual human beings but only social structures.

Let us analyze the implications Blau's dichotomous representation of criminal behavior has for ecological inquiry. First, Blau states that the first question (i.e., the psychological question) conceptualizes crime as behavior engaged by individuals. Can this be otherwise? Note that Blau is referring to violent crime (e.g., rape, murder) and thus we can dispense with notions of organizational actors as perpetrators of "white-collar" crimes. Of course individuals engage in crime. More than that, they commit the very crimes that make up the aggregate crime rate. For example, Blau and Blau (1982) analyze variations in aggregate violent crime rates across SMSAs. The crime rate is simply the number of reported offenses in an area per 100,000 persons. Are we then to conceptualize crime as behavior engaged in by SMSAs? Clearly the aggregate crime rate is inextricably linked to the behavior of individuals and groups within the social unit. Yet it *is* a legitimate and different question to ask why one city has a higher crime rate than another city, rather than why some individuals commit crime and others do not. All this seems obvious enough, so what is the confusion? The problem for Blau's question seems to be that the answer may depend on the differential characteristics of individuals living in different cities, *or* on the social structural conditions in cities independent of individual characteristics, or perhaps most likely a combination of both. In short, misspecification error (or omitted variable bias) and measurement error affect both sociological and psychological investigation. An apparent psychological effect may be due to unmeasured community characteristics correlated with individual characteristics. Likewise, an apparent ecological effect may be due to selective aggregation of individuals into communities. Or, it may be that individual-level processes mediate the effects of more distant macrosociological factors. It seems that recent ecological researchers have assumed that utilization of aggregate units per se guarantees the ultimate demonstration of "macrosociological" effects.

The fallacy of assuming global or structural effects on the basis of the unit of analysis has been noted by organizational researchers. Lincoln and Zeitz's (1980: 392) discussion of aggregation issues in the sociology of organizations parallels issues relevant to the study of communities and crime:

> Questions concerning the locus of causation may legitimately be raised when organizational properties are measured with global indicators not derived from, nor disaggregable to, individual characteristics. In the case of aggregate measures, the analogous indicator at the individual level is readily apparent since its distribution is the raw material from which the organizational measure is derived. But the fact that a global measure does not have an immediately evident or accessible microcounterpart does not make it immune to questions concerning the level at which one's theoretical explanations should be pitched.

In other words, the level at which a causal relation occurs is a complex issue that is not solved simply by the nature of how variables are measured or the unit for which they are measured, since psychological and/or sociological causal factors may underlie relations observed at both the individual and aggregate level of analysis. Thus it is not the unit of analysis that necessarily defines disciplinary boundaries, but the exogenous or intervening mechanisms hypothesized to account for the phenomenon at hand. By restricting the scope of sociological analysis to aggregate units, Blau's position ironically implies that structural factors cannot affect individual behavior, since he defines the latter to be in the realm of psychology. More important, aggregate data are not magical and do not possess strictly macrosociological wisdom as some recent articles would have us believe. Indeed, by relying on aggregate crime rates to represent all that is social about crime, one runs the risk of confounding individual with structural effects. The following section briefly examines one aspect of this issue concerning the aggregate crime rate.

ECOLOGICAL ANALYSIS: PROBLEMS OF INTERPRETATION

An established finding of criminological research is that for serious personal crimes (e.g., homicide, robbery), blacks have offending rates several times those of whites (see, e.g., Hindelang, 1978, 1980, 1981). For example, Hindelang (1981) calculated age-race-sex-specific offending rates for the United States using both Uniform Crime Reports (UCR) and the National Crime Survey (NCS) victim surveys. Compatibility between UCR and NCS estimates was extremely high, particularly for robbery (see also Hindelang, 1978). Regardless of the data source, black males exhibited robbery offending rates anywhere from 9 to 14 times greater than those of whites. For instance, the ratio of black/white robbery offending for adult males (21 and over) is estimated at 14.3 using UCR data and 13.0 using NCS data (Hindelang, 1981: 468). Because of the congruence in data sources, Hindelang concludes that for serious personal crimes at least, large race differentials in arrest rates reflect differential involvement in offending. Recent research (Blumstein and Graddy, 1982) tends to suggest that this differential involvement stems primarily from differences in prevalence of offending and not to differences in individual crime rates (i.e., intensity of offending) among active offenders. That is, a higher proportion of blacks than whites come to be involved in serious criminality, but once engaged, blacks and whites tend to have similar recidivism rates.

The higher individual-level prevalence of offending among blacks than whites has consequences for aggregate analysis. Quite simply, we would expect a positive relationship between percentage black and the aggregate crime rate across areas, controlling for population size. This result is expected because extremely high black offending rates, compared to whites, will induce a positive correlation between percentage black and crimes when standardized by the entire population. What is crucial, however, is that this aggregate correlation does not necessarily tell us anything about the *contextual* effect of racial composition on race-specific offending. It is possible that black offending rates are unrelated, positively related, or even negatively related to percentage black. Each one of the possibilities is consistent with a positive effect of percentage black on aggregate crime.

Consider, for example, two cities with an equivalent size population of 100,000 persons. Assume that the black offending rate in both cities is five times that of whites. For the sake of argument we assume that this rate differential is due to prevalence (p) and not incidence (i). In this hypothetical case, assume that 1% of whites and 5% of blacks were observed to commit one crime in the observation year in each city. To compute race-specific offending rates we need only the racial composition of the aggregate units. Accordingly, let p = .01 for whites and .05 for blacks, with i = 1 for both races. Let City A have 20% blacks and City B 70% blacks (e.g., proportions similar to Pittsburgh and Washington, D.C.). The black offending rate is thus 5,000 per 100,000 in City A and City B. The white offending rate in each city is 1,000 per 100,000. Hence as constrained by the prevalence assumption, black rates are 5 times those of whites.

Note that we are assuming that there is no ecological effect of racial composition on race-specific offending in this example. However, when we compute the aggregate rate, as employed in past research, we find that the offending rate in City B is double that of City A (3,800 versus 1,800), resulting in a positive relationship between percentage black and crime. This is simply because City B contains 50,000 more blacks than City A, even though the black populations of both cities have an equivalent offending rate. To further illustrate the much greater sensitivity of aggregate crime rate to compositional rather than contextual effects, suppose the offending rate of blacks in City A is in fact two times higher than the offending rate of blacks in City B. Even in this case percentage black would be *inversely* related to black offending but still *positively* related to aggregate crime rate (3,800 versus 2,800). Moreover, the tremendous difference in prevalence of offending between races would maintain these relationships in the multivariate case as well.

The use of aggregate crime rate has obvious implications for ecological inquiry. The most important is that the aggregate rate obscures ecological or contextual effects with compositional effects arising from individual-level differences. In the above example percentage black was positively related to aggregate crime, but only because of black-white differences in offending. Recall that Blau (1981: 171) argued (a) racial composition is a characteristic of collectivities, not individuals and (b) analysis of aggregate crime leads to explanations of violence "in terms of the structural conditions promoting conflict." Indeed, there can be little doubt that racial composition represents a structural or macrosocial property of residential environment. The experience of growing up black in a predominantly white community is certainly different than growing up black in a predominantly black community. An entire class of sociological theory is built around the effects of social structure on minority-majority and intergroup relations (see, e.g., Blalock, 1967; Blau, 1977). But racial composition also reflects compositional effects if individual-level racial differences are not taken into account. Hence use of ecological units per se does not necessarily imply a macrosocial perspective. Indeed, much of what is commonly referred to as ecological criminology resembles little that is actually ecological or contextual in perspective. As Kornhauser (1978: 104) bluntly asks delinquency researchers:

> How do we know that area differences in delinquency rates result from the aggregate characteristics of communities rather than the characteristics of individuals selectively aggregated into communities? How do we even know that there are differences at all once their differing composition is taken into account?

Kornhauser's question poses serious problems for the ecological researcher. For example, Messner (1983a) finds a positive direct effect of percentage black on the aggregate homicide rate for SMSAs and claims support for the subculture of violence thesis. Is Messner's finding indicative of a macrosociological effect of racial composition? Since he used the ecological approach (Blau, 1981) we might be inclined to think so. But as shown above, the aggregate crime rate shows gross insensitivity to contextual interpretation. Messner's aggregate finding probably reveals little more than that blacks have a higher offending rate than whites, an effect not clearly attributable to city-level causal factors.

Consequently, it seems that a true test of "macrosociological" effects of racial composition and other structural factors requires that established correlates of criminal behavior be taken into account. As Hindelang's research has shown, there are extremely strong differentials in offending not only by race, but sex and age as well. As Hindelang (1981: 472) notes, the variability in criminality explained by these characteristics is so great that it is incumbent on sociological researchers to take them into account. This does not imply that we must construct or call upon extant social theory to explain demographic correlates such as age (Hirschi and Gottfredson, 1983), but rather that we do not attribute to social structure what may be the manifestations of individual-level processes.

Following Hindelang's logic, some of the truly interesting theoretical questions pertain to the contextual effects of racial composition and other ecological characteristics on offending rates for groups homogeneous on individual-level predictors of involvement in criminality. For example, one important question is the extent to which racial composition has an effect on age-race-sex-specific offending rates. This does not imply that aggregate crime rates are useless. If we are only interested in the effects of strictly "ecological" variables (e.g., structural density, geographical location) then introducing aggregate-level controls for population compositional variables is probably sufficient (Bryne, 1983). But to the extent we are interested in the causal effects of city population and economic structure (e.g., racial composition, economic status, family disorganization) on crime rates we must take into account relevant individual and familial-level characteristics.

Few studies have been conducted in criminology within a contextual framework. This is not for a complete lack of effort or insight, however. Data on *both* individual and aggregate characteristics across a sample of areas that vary on key variables are indeed difficult to obtain. Most contextual studies have been done with self-reported delinquency data, and have been concerned with one issue—the relative effect of aggregate and individual SES. Braithwaite (1979) summarizes the few contextual studies (e.g., Reiss and Rhodes, 1961; Clark and Wenninger, 1962) and concludes that delinquency rates of poor boys are higher in poor slums than in class-mixed areas, which tends to support mainstream poverty theories such as Shaw and McKay. Official arrest data across jurisdictions usually do not contain information on individual income or educational status, and thus have not been able to address such questions. Since self-report data generally yield information confined predominantly to relatively minor infractions, and then only for juveniles, evidence regarding contextual effects of ecological characteristics on homicide, robbery, and other serious crime is quite limited. Perhaps more important, self-report delinquency research has not rigorously explored the causal contextual effects of community characteristics other than poverty.

In sum, only by controlling (or approximately controlling) for individual-level characteristics by which aggregate units differ in their composition will we be in a position reasonably to infer ecological effects. For "pure" ecological variables (e.g., density) that do not have an individual analog it may be that disaggregating the crime rate is not all that important. There is no a priori evidence that population density, for example, differentially influences age-race-sex-specific offending (although it may well). There is, however, a strong possibility that composition variables such as race and economic status, which clearly affect aggregate rates, may also have important contextual effects on demographic-specific offending rates, and that those effects will be different for different demographic subgroups. In the latter portion of this chapter I will discuss empirical strategies to address these contextual questions.

TOWARD A COMMUNITY-LEVEL THEORY OF SOCIAL CONTROL

Another problematic area in the study of communities and crime is the lack of theoretical development in recent years. What we have seen basically are reapplications and extensions of subcultural theory and strain theory. In particular, Messner (1983) and others (see, e.g., Rosenfeld, 1984) have concentrated on testing subcultural theory, while Blau and Blau (1982) have led the revitalization of relative deprivation theory ala Merton. While these perspectives might be quite important, alternative theoretical agendas have been neglected. This section attempts to present the framework of a theoretical model that has as its center not race and class, but community social controls.

In what is probably the most exhaustive review of delinquency theories in many years, Kornhauser (1978) concludes that Shaw and McKay's theory is basically a community-level control theory. In Kornhauser's explication of the Shaw and McKay model, the ecological segregation of communities characterized by low economic status, heterogeneity, and mobility results in ineffective culture and social structure, which in turn leads to weak controls that account for delinquency. Generally speaking, the social disorganization of an area refers to the community's ability to realize its common values (1978: 63). Implicit in this conception is the assumption that communities (and society at large) form a consensus on such basic human values as health, life, order, economic sufficiency, education, and family stability. Since Shaw and McKay showed that crime rates were correlated with the occurrence of other social problems such as truancy, economic dependency, and mental disorders, Kornhauser suggests that such communities were unable to implement and express the true values of their residents. In contrast to subcultural perspectives, it is the inability to realize common values that is the underlying cause of delinquency, not variation in the content of values defining what is morally valid.

Kornhauser's (1978: 83-138) review of the ecological literature indicates that many studies support the findings that crime is concentrated in areas characterized by low economic status, heterogeneity, and residential mobility. However, recently emerging research on juvenile delinquency (Simcha-Fagan and Sampson, 1982) and victimization (Sampson, 1983a) reveals that family disorganization (e.g., percentage divorced, percentage female-headed families) has stronger effects on crime and delinquency than economic status or racial composition. Other research by Sampson (1983a, 1983b) also indicates that the structural density of the physical environment (e.g., percentage of multiple-dwelling units) has a direct effect on victimization rates, independent of mobility, economic level, racial composition, and other neighborhood characteristics.

Despite the number of aggregate-level empirical findings, Kornhauser notes that criminologists have done little to account for the variables that *mediate* the effect of community characteristics: "Neither Shaw and McKay nor those who succeeded them have systematically investigated the variables that link aggregate characteristics of communities and delinquency" (1978: 138). Unfortunately, then, much of the theorizing in the ecological arena has rested on conjecture and speculation.

Kornhauser (1978) has presented a beginning attempt to formalize a theory of community social control that explicitly takes into account intervening processes. She focuses largely on the effects of economic status, heterogeneity, and mobility on formal community controls. The following section extends and modifies her theory in two ways. First, I focus less on economic status and more on the dimensions of family disorganization, mobility, and density. Second, I attempt to specify some of the mediating effects of informal rather than formal social control. The main thesis is that the independent social effects (i.e., independent of individual characteristics) of neighborhood characteristics on delinquency are transmitted primarily through the capacity of a community to exercise informal social controls.

As Kornhauser (1978) has consistently emphasized, social control refers to the ability of a community to realize common values. Janowitz (1975) has noted that scholars often mistakenly equate social control with social repression, socialization, and conformity. According to Janowitz, in the most fundamental sense social control refers to the capacity of a society to regulate itself according to desired principles and values (1975: 82). The opposite of social control can be thought of as coercive control, where a society or community relies predominantly on force and repression to ensure conformity. Perhaps the equation of social control with social repression has been the reason many criminologists link social control theories of deviance (such as Hirschi's, 1969) with conservative ideology (see, e.g., Bookin-Weiner and Horowitz, 1983; Taylor et al., 1973). But, as Janowitz argues, the original meaning of social control is tied to the efforts of individuals, groups, institutions, and communities to realize *collective* (as opposed to forced) goals (1975: 87). Given this conception of social control, the sociological task is to identify and quantify the effect of variables that facilitate or hinder the group pursuit of collective moral goals (1975: 88). Janowitz emphasizes that social control does not rest exclusively on *normative* conceptions of social organization and society. Instead, Janowitz (1975: 88) argues that "the continuing relevance of social control theory reflects the fact that its assumptions and variables incorporate the ecological, technological, economic, and institutional dimensions of social organization." Hence social control theory is concerned not just with conformity or "internalization of norms" (see Empey, 1978: 230-232), but with the external efforts of collectivities to achieve common interests.

Weak social controls take many forms but can generally be classified into two types—formal and informal. Although incorporating both types of social control in her model, Kornhauser places great emphasis on the functioning of formal institutions (e.g., school, community organizations, police) in regulating human behavior and preventing delinquency. As she notes, "Social disorganization produces weak institutional controls, which loosen the constraints on deviating from conventional values" (1979: 31). For example, in Kornhauser's (1978: 73) model the effects of low economic status, heterogeneity, and mobility are hypothesized to result in inadequate institutional resources, isolation of institutions, institutional instability, institutional incapacity to provide routes to valued goals, and institutional discontinuities in socialization and control.

For both Kornhauser and Shaw and McKay, poverty is the prime determinant of the inability of community institutions to provide an effective system of formal social controls. Parallel to the case for individual delinquency, poverty has long been a "master" variable in ecological research. Yet the fact that recent research reveals a relatively weak direct effect on poverty on both official crime and victimization rates (see, e.g., Sampson, 1983b; Messner, 1982) raises some questions regarding the role of economic status in impeding efforts at community social control. Is poverty in fact the most important determinant of the lack of institutional resources, institutional instability, and overall institutional ineffectiveness? If so, do the latter represent the most relevant type of social control in today's society with respect to delinquency? A brief review of community literature in the following section indicates that the increasing bureaucratization, urbanization, and differentiation of modern society has transformed the nature of formal institutions, rendering them less autonomous in their capacity for social control. As a result, the evidence suggests that *informal* social control has assumed increased importance in today's society. The following section examines how the changing nature of community has reduced the effect of ecological characteristics on formal social controls.

THE CHANGING NATURE OF COMMUNITY

One of the underlying assumptions of Kornhauser's (1978) community control model is that territorial communities are the basis of collective action. Social disorganization is thus defined as the inability of the community to act together to realize common values. However, Tilly (1973) and others have raised a pointed and troubling question: Do communities act? Tilly's review suggests that communities have been transformed into extralocal and national networks of power and communication. By focusing exclusively on territorial communities, Tilly (1973: 212) argues that classical urbanization theorists failed to notice the nonterritorial relations that have replaced them. In particular, modern communication and transportation systems have transformed institutional relations, divorcing them from spatial considerations. While formal institutions may be located in and provide services to local communities, they are in large part controlled by city, state, and national networks of power.

Duffee's (1980) analysis of the community context of criminal justice in America supports these observations. Following Warren (1978), Duffee (1980: 152) describes the vertical dimension of community structure as the extent to which a local social unit is tied to or dependent on a nonlocal system for performance of its locality-relevant functions. In contrast, the horizontal dimensions of community refers to the degree to which various groups, organizations, and systems *within* a community are interrelated for the performance of community functions (1980: 152). Communities that depend on higher governmental structures for the performance of formal social control functions are influenced by a relative strong vertical dimension. Although communities exhibit both vertical and horizontal dimensions, Duffee's (1980: 153) summary is clear: "The major conclusion from observing contemporary American communities is that the horizontal dimension has tended to weaken and the vertical dimension has tended to strengthen dramatically in the last fifty years." Similar to Tilly, Duffee argues that industrialization, urbanization, and bureaucratization are the predominant forces that have tended to make communities dependent on vertical linkages for performance of social control functions, hence making communities less autonomous. In commenting on the transference of power from the community to extralocal structures, Duffee (1980: 153) concludes:

> Social control functions are increasingly state and federal concerns, as are many social participation and mutual support activities. This trend has tended to mean that various local units charged with the delivery stages of different functional activities have less in common with each other, or to local citizenry, than to superstructures at the state and national levels to which they belong.

In short, the evidence suggests that communities have declined in the sense of serving as the basis for indigenous collective action to realize common values. The changing nature of community has obvious implications for the role of formal institutions in organizing to prevent delinquency. As Tilly (1973) notes, "deliberate community organization as a tactic for engineering change is only likely to work under an unusual set of conditions." Such conditions rarely arise in the case of delinquency prevention. Indeed, how can a community realize common goals through collective institutional action when exogenous factors control the very institutions located in the community? The argument being presented does not deny the importance of formal social controls in preventing delinquency. Rather, the main point is that in a modern, differentiated society, indigenous community characteristics have attenuated effects on social controls exerted by formal institutions, many of which have vertical linkages to *outside* the community. In other words, much of the variation in formal social controls is determined by larger community, interurban, state, and national forces rather than by neighborhood characteristics. In contrast, there is much evidence to suggest that the community has strong influences on *informal* social control.

INFORMAL SOCIAL CONTROL

A community-oriented approach to informal social controls rests on the assumption that the only truly effective means of maintaining public norms is by neighbors assuming responsibility for one another (see Greenberg et al., 1982). Examples of informal social control are neighbors taking note of and questioning strangers, watching over each other's property, assuming responsibility for supervision of youth activities, and intervening in local disturbances. Greenberg et al. have reviewed a wide body of research concerned with identifying what characteristics are associated with the willingness of residents to assume responsibility and intervene in public disturbances. They conclude that the "willingness to intervene is linked with the familiarity, security, and responsibility that are connected with the neighborhood setting. In contrast, residents of neighborhoods where most people are strangers to one another may be no more likely to intervene there than in an unfamiliar location" (1982: 9). This supports Fischer's (1981) distinction between the public and private spheres of city life. While urbanization may not negatively affect interpersonal ties with friends and personal associates, it does tend to produce fear, distrust, and unwillingness to intervene in public encounters. At the intraurban level, Fischer's thesis suggests that neighborhood characteristics will have a stronger effect on the public sphere of life noted by Greenberg et al. than on the private world of interpersonal relations.

For example, structural density seems to have direct implications for neighborhood settings of familiarity, security, and responsibility. Sampson (1983b) argues that as structural density increases the capacity for guardianship is decreased, and thus security and familiarity are hindered. Multiple-dwelling unit structures offer increased criminal opportunities while reducing surveillance capabilities. Moreover, even when surveillance is physically possible, Newman (1972) argues that as the number of households sharing common living space increases, residents are less able to recognize neighbors, to be concerned for them, and to engage in guardianship activities (see also Roncek, 1981: 88). By increasing anonymity while decreasing effective means of surveillance, structural density serves to impede informal social control.

Residential mobility also has implications for informal neighborhood social control. A neighborhood with high population turnover has a greater proportion of residents who are strangers to one another than areas with a stable, long-term population. As Greenberg et al.'s (1982) research shows, residents are least likely to intervene in a crime incident when it occurs in the context of an anonymous setting with strangers. Residents are also less likely to assume guardianship responsibilities for their neighbors when they hardly know them. Thus informal social control activities such as watching over neighborhood property, taking note of neighborhood activities, and intervening in local disturbances are likely to be impeded by neighborhood residential mobility.

Residential mobility has also been shown to affect adversely community attachment and local social bonds, which are closely linked to Greenberg et al.'s (1982) notion of responsibility. Kasarda and Janowitz (1974) tested a systemic model of community that examined formal and informal networks of social control. As Kasarda and Janowitz (1974: 329) explain:

> In the systemic model, community organization is treated as an essential aspect of mass society. It is a structure which has ecological, institutional, and normative dimensions. The local community is viewed as a complex system of friendship and kinship networks and formal and informal association ties rooted in family life and ongoing socialization processes.

Kasarda and Janowitz's systemic model posits residential mobility as the key exogenous factor influencing community behaviors and attitudes. The major intervening variables are friendship and kinship bonds and formal and informal associational ties within the local community. They argue that "residential mobility operates as a barrier to the development of extensive friendship and kinship bonds and widespread local associational ties" (1974: 330). Kasarda and Janowitz's empirical analysis supported the systemic model. They found that length of residence was the strongest positive predictor of local social bonds and community attachment. When length of residence increases, so does attachment to area, identification and feelings of responsibility for one's neighborhood, and informal networks of friends. In fact, Kasarda and Janowitz (1974: 336) found that residential mobility alone explained more of the variance in local social bonds and community sentiments than did the combined effects of population size, density, social class, and stage in life cycle.

Although Kasarda and Janowitz did not operationalize measures of family structure, their theoretical orientation suggests that family disorganization also has negative consequences for community social bonds. The cornerstone of their perspective is that the local community is a complex system of networks "rooted in family life and ongoing socialization processes" (1974: 329). By implication, a breakdown in family ties and the isolation of family from the community would lead to attenuated local social bonds, community sentiment, and organizational participation. Kornhauser (1978) similarly suggests that the family life of a community can have important implications for social organization. She argues that even in the absence of voluntary associations, stable families are able to link youth to the community. Kornhauser (1978: 81, emphasis added) emphasizes the important role that the family plays in the socialization of youth:

> It can provide contacts with economic institutions, aid in doing school work, and knowledge of recreational facilities: it can perform many other functions that link the child to institutions, thus enabling him to employ institutional routes to valued goals and consequently binding him more effectively to conventional institutions. By parent's efforts, *both individual and collective*, nonfamily institutions are made more responsive to the child's needs.

Following Kornhauser's logic, pronounced family disorganization in an area will disrupt what she refers to as the "collective" efforts of families to link neighborhood youth to the wider society.

The informal nature of collective family social control has not often been studied. Indeed, the effects of the family have largely been studied from the viewpoint of "children under the roof." That is, the effect of the behavior of parents is studied only on the delinquency of their own children. But children and adolescents are often supervised, watched, and even reprimanded by other than their own parents. As Skogan and Maxfield (1981: 105) note: "In integrated areas adults keep an eye on children, and the whole community eyes strangers carefully. . . . People with a stake in the community and its future 'police' events there with vigor." Thus in areas with a cohesive family structure (and usually low mobility) parents often take on responsibility not just for their own children, but for other youth in the community as well. The fundamental fact that delinquency is a group phenomenon (see, e.g., Zimring, 1981) may attest to the efficacy of this strategy. By supervising and keeping track of youth other than their own, parents are maintaining some degree of control over group activity that accounts for well over half of all delinquency (Zimring, 1981). Indeed, intervening in group processes (see Short and Strodbeck, 1965) may be the only effective means of controlling delinquency. At a very basic level, two-parent households provide increased supervision, not only for their own property (Cohen and Felson, 1979) but for public activities in the neighborhood. For example, acts such as truancy by local youth are more likely to be noticed, particularly if one parent is home during daytime hours.

In contrast, in an anonymous setting with frequent population turnover and a high proportion of divorces or working single mothers, there is a reduced likelihood of noticing and acting on the truancy and delinquency of neighborhood youth. The informal social control exercised by the community is thus weakened, as youths are free to determine their behavior without the supervision or interference of parents, neighbors, and concerned residents. Cohesive family structures are probably effective not because they are able to intervene in such actual crime and delinquency, but because they are aware of and intervene in group activities (e.g., truancy, "hanging out") that are usually the predecessors of involvement in more serious delinquent activities. There is some empirical support for these notions. Sampson (1983a) showed that of all neighborhood characteristics studied, family disorganization was the strongest predictor of juvenile group offending. That is, juveniles tended to offend in groups more often in neighborhoods characterized by high family disorganization than low family disorganization.

Ironically, further support for this argument is found in the very nature of delinquent activities. The fact that what delinquency does occur in settings of two-parent households and stable populations is concealed attests to the strength of informal neighborhood social controls. Back lots, woods, forts, and basements are often the scene of adolescent delinquency in suburban-type communities, away from the stream of community life. The ubiquitous street life in lower-income, high-density, disorganized urban areas provides a sharp contrast. Groups of youth milling around street corners in midday performing "mildly" delinquent acts such as drinking and gambling is a common sight not likely to elicit much notice. Consider, for example, Rainwater's study of the Pruitt-Igo housing projects in St. Louis, which contained a lower-income, mobile population with a high degree of female-headed households. Rainwater (1970: 276) notes that while children in the middle-upper classes keep their deviant activities secret from parents, adults in the projects ignore children they see engaged in smoking, gambling, and other adultlike behavior. In effect, concealment of deviance is not really necessary because neighborhood standards relate mostly to personalistic rather than public norms (see also Suttles, 1968: 78).

Public displays of drinking, drug taking, graffiti, gambling, and other signs of disorder have been labeled by Hunter (1978) as *incivilities*. The public presence of incivilities sends a signal that not only are "minor" forms of deviance tolerated, but that the scope of neighborhood social control is so weak that new frontiers of deviance are ripe to be explored. Greenberg et al. (1982: 3) argue that incivilities and signs of disorder are expected to result in increased crime and delinquency because youths recognize such deterioration and "assume that residents are so indifferent to what goes on in their neighborhood that they will not be motivated to confront strangers, intervene in a crime, or call the police." Thus the lack of informal social control in a community may have direct effects on individual behavior by creating a context where deviance has free reign. While delinquency can and indeed does occur in stable family areas of single-unit homes (i.e., low structural density), much of it is concealed and out of public view, in itself suggesting that informal social controls are effective. Youths in such a neighborhood may have as much to lose if the neighbors observe their delinquency as if their own parents do. If youths feel or correctly determine that the "eyes of the community" are on them, then they are forced to reduce, eliminate, or conceal their delinquent involvement, lest they risk apprehension. By contrast, if an adolescent's (or more likely a group of adolescents) behavior in high density, mobile, disorganized urban areas does not elicit public attention or action, then he or she (or they) are, to that extent, free to deviate. The norms of informal public social control in the community are simply too weak to bind him or her to conventional behavior.

In summary, the argument developed is that neighborhood characteristics such as family disorganization, residential mobility, and structural density weaken informal social control networks. Specifically, informal social controls are impeded by weak local social bonds, lowered community attachment, anonymity, and reduced capacity for surveillance and guardianship. Other factors such as poverty and racial composition also probably affect informal control, although as argued earlier their influence is in all likelihood indirect. Residents in areas characterized by family disorganization, mobility, and building density are less able to perform guardianship activities (see especially Cohen and Felson, 1979; Cohen et al., 1981), less likely to report general deviance (e.g., incivilities) to authorities, to intervene in public disturbances (see Fischer, 1981), and to assume responsibility for supervision of youth activities. The result is that deviance in general is tolerated and public norms of social control are not effective.

This conception of informal social control does not imply that individual-level controls or institutions of formal social controls (e.g., schools, police) are unimportant. Rather, I am suggesting that consideration of informal community social control in conjunction with personal and institutional controls may add to a fuller understanding of delinquency. Indeed, at the individual level, Hirschi (1969) has already established the importance of attachment to family and school, commitment, involvement, and belief in bonding youth to society. At the community level, Kornhauser (1978) has detailed the institutional instability, isolation of institutions, and inadequate institutional resources that result from low economic status, mobility, and heterogeneity. Given this considerable empirical and theoretical foundation already established at the level of personal and institutional sources of social control, the present chapter has attempted to shed some new light on mechanisms of informal social control. The declining nature of community institutional autonomy outlined earlier seems to give the informal control approach particular relevancy.

DISCUSSION

The theoretical perspective advocated here has several advantages, not the least of which is consistency with recent research on urbanism, neighborhoods, and social networks. Early community social control theorists (Shaw and McKay) and even Kornhauser to a large extent assumed that factors such as low economic status and mobility increased crime by destroying social ties among friends and neighbors in the community, which in turn loosened control networks. That is, the decline in primary relations among people in a community was hypothesized to be a key ingredient underlying weak social controls. This notion is of course similar to the classic Wirthian hypothesis at the urban level. Wirth (1938) argued that the complexity, overstimulation, and density found in the urban environment strained social relations. The urbanite was presumed to be impersonal and superficial, and this estrangement was hypothesized to affect family life and intimate bonds in the community. Similarly, poverty and mobility were hypothesized by Shaw and McKay and Kornhauser to weaken intimate social bonds and interpersonal relations in the community.

Recent research tends to suggest that the Wirthian hypothesis is naive. Social networks and psychological well-being are alive and well in cities (Gans, 1962; Wellman, 1979). As Tilly (1973: 212) notes, "Those who saw decay, eclipse, and disintegration of community life with the growth of cities were probably concentrating too hard on *territorial* communities, and failing to notice the nonterritorial forms which replaced them." The research of network theorists (see, e.g., Granovetter, 1973; Wellman, 1979) has shown that contrary to the assumption of decline in primary relations, modern urbanites have substituted non-spatial communities for spatial communities; metropolitan residents build viable sets of social relations that are dispersed in space (Tilly, 1973: 211). Modern urbanites, for example, may not know their neighborhoods intimately, but they are quite likely to have interpersonal networks spread throughout the city, state, and even across the country (see Wellman, 1979). If urbanization, heterogeneity, and mobility do not have the expected negative affect on intimate social ties, then how do they weaken social controls?

Fischer's (1975, 1983) theory of urbanism provides a means to distinguish conceptually the consequences of community structure for social control. Fischer (1981) makes explicit the distinction between the public and private spheres of social life. In the urban "world of strangers" (Lofland, 1973) the urbanite typically has the capacity to know people categorically, to place them by appearance and behavior in one of many urban subcultures (e.g., age, sex, ethnicity, lifestyle—see also Suttles, 1968). But as Fischer (1981: 307) argues, this is a *situational*, not a psychological, style, and says nothing about attitudes and action in the private sphere. City dwellers have not lost the capacity for "deep, long-lasting, multifaceted relationships," but have gained the capacity for surface, fleeting relationships that are restricted. Consequently, Fischer (1981: 308) argues that "urbanism does not estrange individuals from familiar and similar people. Conversely, urbanism's effects are specified; estrangement occurs in the public sphere—less helpfulness, more conflict—but not in the private one—personal relations and psychological well-being."

Drawing on Fischer's distinctions and applying them to the intraurban level allows us to state explicitly what was implicitly assumed in the theoretical framework above: The effects of neighborhood characteristics on crime and delinquency operate primarily on the public domain of informal social control. Persons in low-income, high-density, high-mobility neighborhoods have friends, kinship networks, and social ties much like their counterparts in well-to-do areas with stable populations, low density, and cohesive family structures. What differs in the former type of environment is the attenuation of *public* social controls exercised by the community at large. This distinction allows for the fact that interpersonal primary relations are often found in ghetto areas where disorganization is supposedly high. Indeed, a fundamental and repeated criticism of disorganization and social control theories has been that slum residents have rich primary relations (see, e.g., Feagin, 1973). But as Kornhauser and Fischer have noted, these sorts of relations pertain to the private world or to small primary groups in neighborhoods, and does not extend to the arena of public norms and the efficacy of social control.

Perhaps without realizing it, other observers have also discovered this basic theme in discussing what it is that most desire in a community.

> When I speak of the concern for "community," I refer to a desire for the observance of standards of right and seemly conduct in the public places in which one lives and moves, those standards to be consistent with—and supportive of—the values and life styles of the particular individual. Around one's home, the places where one shops, and the corridors through which one walks there is for each of us a public space wherein our sense of security, self-esteem, and propriety is either reassured or jeopardized by the people and events we encounter. Viewed this way, the concern for community is less the "need" for "belonging" (or . . . the need

> to overcome feelings of "alienation" or "anomie") than the normal but not compulsive interest of any rationally self-interested person in his and his family's environment [Wilson, 1975: 27].

Indeed, Wilson's observations go right to the heart of Kornhauser's basic position—we do not need communities so much to satisfy our private and interpersonal needs, which are best met elsewhere, but to express and realize common values and standards. In this sense, what a community-level theory of social control has to offer is the specification of the effects that neighborhood characteristics have on the capacity and ability of community residents to implement and maintain public norms.

In sum, the underlying premise of this chapter is that community structure has an affect on criminal behavior that is not fully accounted for by individual characteristics. I think that Fischer (1975) provides the most reasonable statement of the utility of theoretical arguments that hinge on the demonstration of structural effects independent of individual-level characteristics. In accounting for his development of a subcultural theory of urbanism, Fischer acknowledges that nonecological variables (e.g., age, sex, ethnicity) are probably more important than ecological ones in explaining stress and coping behavior. Similarly, delinquency and crime are multidetermined, and the effects of neighborhood characteristics are probably relatively small compared to the effects of such predictors as sex, race, attachment, and so on. If community (or urbanization) effects are small, why study them? A clue is found in Fischer's (1975: 1337) intellectually honest answer:

> The subcultural model does not . . . imply that . . . ecological factors have large, practical, or policy relevant effects. By far the more important influences of behavior are the nonecological ones. The real implication is theoretical.

Indeed, the empirical demonstration of autonomous effects of community structure on criminal behavior would be an important theoretical breakthrough. How large these effects might be remains to be seen. If we are to be honest, though, we should probably admit that the search for such effects is driven by theoretical rather than practical concerns. The following section concludes this essay with an overview of empirical strategies by which we might validate the importance of community in the study of crime and delinquency.

CONCLUSION

It is evident that prior research does not provide us with adequate knowledge of the relationship between community characteristics and processes of informal social control, and of the autonomous effects of neighborhood characteristics on criminal behavior. Despite this somewhat gloomy assessment, there are several empirical strategies that may be fruitfully pursued.

First, analysis of demographically disaggregated arrest rates present a useful alternative to analysis of contextual data, given that the latter are quite rare in criminology. Indeed, data on both individuals and communities across a sample of areas that vary on key characteristics is almost nonexistent. Although arrest data do not provide detailed information on individual-level characteristics, they do provide what Hindelang (1981) has shown to be the strongest individual-level correlates of serious criminal offending—age, race, and sex. Moreover, Hindelang (1981) has demonstrated that UCR arrest data and victimization are quite compatible concerning these correlates for serious personal crimes. Although there are undoubtedly variations in arrest practices across cities, one can explicitly introduce measures to control for differential police effectiveness (e.g., arrest/offense ratios, clearance rate, police per capita). Once these CJS effects are taken into account, Hindelang's research provides a strong basis for assuming that differentials in arrest rates for serious crimes reflect differential involvement in *offending*. Utilizing these assumptions and procedures, Sampson (1984b) analyzed the effects of such city characteristics as poverty, inequality, racial composition, and police arrest probabilities on age-race-sex-specific homicide rates for large U.S. cities. This investigation will, it is hoped, shed light on some of the contextual propositions derived from current theory.

However, we cannot be content merely to analyze arrest and census data, useful though such an adventure might be. By far the most important empirical task seems to be the measurement of the processes that mediate the effect of community characteristics on individual behavior. As Kornhauser's (1978) exhaustive review of ecological research demonstrates, criminologists have for the most part simply *inferred* the existence of intervening processes, even though the correlation of crime with ecological characteristics may be consistent with many different theoretical perspectives. One obvious reason for this tendency is that ecological research overwhelmingly relies on census data, which do not provide measures of the constructs presumed to account for the phenomenon at hand. For example, above I overviewed a theoretical model that posited mediating effects of such processes as guardianship, informal social control, and community attachment. Demonstration of the validity of such a model requires more than just conjecture, it requires empirical validation. Fortunately, inroads are being made in this area, which may bespeak a more rigorous empirical stance on the part of ecologically minded researchers in the future.

7

Sports and Delinquency

RODNEY STARK
LORI KENT
ROGER FINKE

At least since the Duke of Wellington remarked that "the Battle of Waterloo was won on the playing fields of Eton," it has widely been believed that participation in athletics builds character, self-confidence, and discipline. In keeping with this belief, sports have always been a major element in programs aimed at delinquency prevention or at reforming delinquents. Groups such as the Boys Clubs, Police Athletic Leagues, and even the Boy Scouts, explicitly assume a link between athletics and delinquency.

However, in recent years, social scientists, ever-ready to challenge conventional wisdom and traditional values, have reinterpreted the relationship between athletics and delinquency. It isn't that sports help boys go straight, they argue, rather sports simply filter out the delinquent boys. Sheldon Glueck and Eleanor Glueck (1950) claimed that delinquent boys dislike competitive activities and therefore tend to shun organized athletics. In similar style, Yiannakis (1976) argued that delinquents tend to drop out of sports programs. Surely, it would not strain credulity to suppose that coaches might reinforce such tendencies by discouraging or even by cutting boys given to disruptive behavior or with unsavory reputations. If these revisionist notions are correct, then correlations between athletic participation and nondelinquency are not causal, or if they are, the causation runs in the opposite direction (delinquency causes elimination from sports). In this perspective, participation in youth soccer would not *keep* boys straight, but would be taken as an indication that they *are* straight.

Given the widespread belief in the beneficial effects of sports, the huge programs predicated on this belief, and the underlying hostility of many social science researchers to sports, it is strange to find the empirical literature on this question so slight. But the journals are nearly empty of satisfactory data. Indeed, we could locate only two worthwhile empirical studies.

Schafer (1969) reported a negative correlation between sports participation and delinquency. However, when he controlled for class the correlation vanished except among low-achieving boys from blue-collar homes. Even if the effect of sports is this limited, it still is significant since these are the most delinquency-prone boys. However, Schafer lacked data to untangle the causal order—did athletics recruit the good boys from this subgroup, or did it make or keep them good? In addition, Schafer's data are limited to two high schools in the Midwest.

The second study, Landers and Landers (1978), also reported a correlation between athletics and nondelinquency. Moreover, all extracurricular activities had this effect. And, boys active both in sports and in other extracurriculars were the least delinquent group. Once again, the study cannot assess causal order and its data base is quite limited. The research was done on one high school in a northeastern town of 7,800. In many such towns high school sports are the focus of intense community pride that, in turn, could lead to the efficient elimination of all the "bad apples" who might disgrace the team and the town. Moreover, boys active in both sports and extracurriculars are members of any school's social elite (regardless of their family status) and it is well-known that such boys are low on delinquency (Hirschi, 1969).

What is needed is research based on larger, more representative samples, and that includes the data needed to sort out causal order—to see if sports reduce delinquency or merely recruit nondelinquents. Ideally, a longitudinal study is required.

Fortunately, a high-quality longitudinal data set, based on a national cluster sample of males, recently became available through the data archive of Survey Research Center at the University of Michigan. The study was designed and directed by Jerald Bachman (Bachman et al., 1967). The data are of high quality and of great scope. More then 2,000 tenth grade boys were drawn in the sample in 1966. They were then reinterviewed over an eight-year period—five waves of data collection—the last time when most of these males were 24. Data on delinquency were collected in all waves of the study, but only in the third wave (in the spring of the boy's senior year in high school) were data on sports participation collected. These data cover all forms of organized athletic participation.

MEASURES OF DELINQUENCY

The data set includes a number of measures of delinquency. Each is based on self-report items. It is necessary to use these measures as they were constructed and scored by the Michigan researchers because almost all of the individual items have been omitted from the data tapes made available to outside researchers. We have based our analysis on six delinquency indices. The first is based on school delinquency and includes questions on truancy, expulsion, hitting a teacher, and the like. The second is based on a question about running away from home. The third is an index of trouble with parents and includes items on hitting parents and family conflict. These three measures deal primarily with status offenses, acts that are illegal only when committed by minors. For example, it is not illegal for adults to skip school or leave home without permission.

The three measures of delinquency concentrate on crime—acts that are illegal at any age. The first of these is an index of serious delinquency, which includes a range of items from arson, assault with a weapon, and auto-theft to shoplifting and petty theft. The second measures acts of interpersonal aggression, such as beating up on someone so badly that they require medical treatment. The final measure is an index of acts of theft and vandalism. Generally speaking, the acts of delinquency reported by these boys were clustered at the least serious end of each index. Fewer than 5% admitted to arson or assault with a weapon, whereas 46% admitted the theft of an item worth less than $50 (at age 16).

Sports participation was indexed on the basis of the number of organized sports in which a boy participated during his senior year in high school. Internal analysis revealed no differential sports effects. That is, the effects of playing football were similar to those for playing basketball, baseball, and other sports.

SEARCHING FOR SPORTS EFFECTS

Since the data on athletic participation were gathered in the third wave of the study, administered in the spring of the sample's senior year, the most appropriate starting point was to examine the impact of athletics on delinquency data also collected that year. Table 7.1 shows

TABLE 7.1 Correlations Between Athletic Participation and Delinquency Among Seniors

	Correlations (r) with Athletic Participation during High School	
Status Offenses		
School delinquency	−.07	(.003)
Running away	.00	(NS)
Trouble with parents	.00	(NS)
Crime		
Index of serious delinquency	.00	(NS)
Interpersonal aggression	.02	(NS)
Theft and vandalism	.03	(NS)

NOTE: NS = not significant.

the correlations between playing team sports in high school and delinquent behavior during a boy's last year in school. Frankly, the results astonished us. There simply are no sports effects to be seen. Granted, there is one tiny (but significant) correlation suggesting that athletes are less likely to commit acts of school delinquency. But this could be a purely random result since six independent measures of delinquency were examined, as shown in the table. For the remainder of the delinquency measures, the findings are nil.

Faced with these results, we suspected we would have no reason to pursue the longitudinal potential of the data. For if, as it appeared, athletics are not correlated with nondelinquency, the question of whether sports makes boys "good" or recruits "good" boys is wholly moot: It would seem to do neither.

However, we suspected the zero-order correlations might be masking interaction effects. Therefore, we introduced a series of control variables. Immediately we stumbled on to a stunning, if somewhat curious, interaction. Athletic participation seems to have no effect on delinquency of white males. But it seems to have potent effects on blacks. Even more surprising, the effects appeared to be in the wrong direction. That is, we found that among blacks, athletes were more likely than nonathletes to be delinquent.

The introduction of class controls added to the puzzle. First of all, contrary to Schafer's (1969) results, no relationship appeared even for working-class whites. But class had effects among blacks. Although we had only a small number of middle- and upper-class blacks (30) to work with, the relationships between athletics and delinquency were negative among them. Indeed, three of the six relationships were significant at the .07 level or above. Not only was this opposite from Schafer's findings for whites, it still left the strikingly positive correlations among the largest group of blacks.

We then turned to the longitudinal data in an attempt to discover the meaning of these findings. We still found no effects among whites. But the black picture not only clarified greatly; it spelled out an intriguing message: Reform.

THE REFORMATION OF BLACK ATHLETES

The first question that arises is, if black athletes are more delinquent than nonathletes at age 18, what were they like at 16? The answer can be seen in Table 7.2. The correlations between athletic participation and delinquency are much stronger at age 16 than at age 18. Sixteen-year-old black males who took part in school sports were much more likely than blacks who did not join teams to commit acts of school delinquency, to run away from home, to report serious trouble with their parents, to be high on the index of serious delinquency, to score high on interpersonal aggression, and on theft and vandalism. Thus athletes were not simply worse in some ways, but worse across the board. Notice, however, what has happened by age 18. All of the correlations are much smaller, and three of them no longer significant. Thus black athletes were much less likely to stand out on delinquency after participating in school athletics than before. This strongly suggests that, among blacks, athletes are not a selection of the best-behaved boys, but are overselected from the worse behaved. That is, black athletes stand out on delinquency, perhaps because they represent the most energetic, boldest, rowdiest, and possibly even the most ambitious young males. So much, then, for the "selection of non-delinquent" hypotheses advanced by some social scientists. Moreover, having overrecruited delinquent blacks, sports seem to have a markedly beneficial effect on their behavior. They become less different from other blacks in terms of their delinquency as they pass through high school.

But this is not the end of the story. Does sports participation have lasting impact on black males? The answer clearly is yes. When these young men were 24, they were restudied. Several of the same sets of delinquency measures were reasked then (those devoted to status offenses were dropped since they do not apply to adults). Once again, black athletes are different from nonathletes. But now they are less likely to commit offenses. While two of the indices fall short of usual standards

TABLE 7.2 Longitudinal Effects of Athletics on Delinquency Among Black Males

	Correlations (r) with Athletic Participation during High School					
	At Age 16		*At Age 18*		*At Age 24*	
Status Offenses						
School delinquency	.21	(.02)	.04	(NS)	–	–
Running away	.30	(.003)	.28	(.002)	–	–
Trouble with parents	.32	(.002)	.19	(.03)	–	–
Crime						
Index of serious delinquency	.17	(.05)	.09	(NS)	–.17	(.05)
Interpersonal aggression	.15	(.09)	.10	(NS)	–.11	(.14)
Theft and vandalism	.17	(.05)	.14	(.08)	–.11	(.14)

NOTE: NS = not significant.

of statistical significance, all three correlations have negative signs. Moreover, if controls are added for the level of delinquency for each boy at 18, then all three adult negative correlations rise sharply and each is very significant statistically.

Thus a very coherent picture of quite impressive and important athletic effects on delinquency shows up for blacks in the longitudinal data. It is the most, not the least, delinquent blacks who go into high school sports. By the time they are near the end of their senior year these black athletes are only slightly more delinquent than their nonathletic peers. And by the time they are adults of 24, black athletes are less likely to violate the law than are their nonathletic peers. Such a pattern ought not be called a prevention program. Rather, high school sports seem to achieve a considerable degree of reform.

WHY ARE SPORTS EFFECTS LIMITED TO BLACKS?

While our longitudinal findings are quite dramatic, they also raise a serious question: Why are blacks so positively affected by sports participation, while whites are not affected at all?

One suggestion we considered was that black athletes are more likely than nonathletes to go to college, and it was college attendance, not sports, that reformed them. But this answer fails in a number of ways. First, considerable reform of black athletes took place in high school. Second, college attendance had no impact on the adult conformity of juvenile offenders—not among blacks or among whites (Stark et al., forthcoming).

The answer to this question lies, in our judgment, in the greater salience of sports in the black than in the white community; that sports have only a reforming affect as they are the focus of a socially integrated community. In prior research we have discovered that this is the way in which religious commitment also serves to diminish delinquency—only in communities where the majority are church members are individual-level correlations found between religiousness and delinquency (Stark et al., 1981).

For a long time, athletics was one of the few plausible roads to fame and fortune for blacks in America. Even today, not only are professional athletes very disproportionately black, but athletes make up a very disproportionate number of wealthy and famous blacks. This both reflects and further encourages a much higher proportion of young blacks than young whites to aspire to be athletes and to make serious efforts to succeed in sports. This suggests several things. First of all, once into sports, blacks may not only try harder to make the team, but to model their behavior on the basis of sport's ideology—since sports builds character, an aspiring athlete ought to be of good character. Indeed, blacks may try harder to earn the good opinion of their coaches. But we suspect a second major phenomenon is at work here. If the black community is generally more interested in sports, then black athletes will receive greater attention and admiration from their peers and from the community-at-large than will white athletes. Consequently, sports may have powerful effects on the self-esteem and aspirations of black athletes—factors well-known for their potent effects on delinquency (Hirschi, 1969).

Several aspects of the data support this view. First, when the study was conducted mandatory busing had not begun. Thus our black respondents were not scattered in integrated schools—75% were concentrated in all black or nearly all black schools. That is, they were in schools that could serve as a focal point for a local black community. Second, students in the black high schools accorded considerably higher prestige to student athletes than did students in white high schools. Indeed, that the black schools frequently competed against white schools could have increased the salience of high schools sports as a source of pride and solidarity in black communities.

If this interpretation is correct—if the black effects are produced by community involvement in high school sports—then similar effects should exist for some whites. Sports ought to influence conformity for whites living in small communities intensely involved in high school sports. That is, where the conditions of athletic participation are similar, the results ought to be similar. Keep in mind that one (and possibly both) of the studies reporting a negative correlation between athletics and delinquency was based on small town data. To pursue this hypothesis it was necessary to isolate a subset of white respondents: those enrolled in small town high schools, especially those far from major cities, and where local teams inspire intense community concern.

SMALL TOWN STARS

The task of isolating the proper schools was complex. We wanted schools that met a number of criteria. First of all, they had to be in places far enough from metropolitan centers so that they rely on their own news media. In communities served by major metropolitan newspapers and blanketed by big city radio and TV, high school sports are submerged from public view. The exploits of local teams are ignored by these outside media, which devote their coverage to professional teams, to national sports stories, and to the teams of the nearest major universities. In addition, for high school athletes to be the focus of public attention there also must exist a concentrated community. Hence we excluded some schools because they were consolidated schools located in a crossroads village and serving a large rural area from which students were bused. Our aim, therefore, was for smaller communities far from a major metropolitan center. But not all such towns are sports oriented. Those that are not ought not produce effects similar to those we have found among blacks, for, in our judgment, athletics produce conformity only to the extent that a network of people invest sports with the capacity to create serious stakes in conformity. Where people do not accord athletes high respect and impose stricter standards of behavior and surveillance upon them, the effects will not be forthcoming.

Recall that we are using a cluster sample made up of 87 high schools. Since respondents were asked about the relative social standing of various kinds of students, including athletes, it is possible to limit our selection to schools well above average in according high status to athletes. In this way we separated the more or less sports-oriented communities. Other problems were not so easily solved.

For reasons we do not fully comprehend, the original investigators refuse to release the names of the schools in the sample, the towns they are in, or even the name of the state in which they are located. Some of this information could be inferred from available data. Thus, for example, since we have data on the state of birth of each boy, it is easy to locate schools by state—surely none would have a modal state of birth other than that in which it was located. We also have data on the size of the community in which respondents grew up. Hence we could eliminate all schools in which students mostly grew up in major-sized cities. Others could be excluded because too many boys grew up in major cities, thus indicating that the school is near a suburb. Others were excluded because all or nearly all of the students grew up in rural areas, thus indicating a consolidated rural school. We also eliminated schools with a significant nonwhite enrollment.

Of course, the kinds of places we were searching for are not any longer typical of American life. In the end we had to settle for only 11 schools, and a sample of 161 boys. Each was enrolled in a sports-oriented school in a modest-sized community.

Table 7.3 shows our results. Clearly, the data closely resemble findings for blacks. While unlike blacks, white athletes in small town America are not more delinquent than nonathletes at age 16, they are, for the most part, no less delinquent than nonathletes. However, by age 18 this pattern has changed dramatically. Relative to nonathletes, the athletes have become very markedly and significantly less delinquent on all six measures. Moreover, as with blacks, the conformity effects of athletes last. At age 24, the athletes are significantly less likely to break the law.

Thus it seems clear that in both sets of findings the recruitment-of-conformists hypothesis is rejected. Sports, when they are correlated with conformity, do not select good boys, but instead seem to make boys better. Where sports fail to have this effect on youth is where sports, or at least high school sports, do not count for enough. If sports are failing most white teenagers, it is because big cities and the mass media have reduced the significance of being a high school star.

CONCLUSION

Since much of our recent work on crime and delinquency has focused on religious effects, it might seem a major departure for us to have turned our attention to the effects of sports participation. Yet we suspected an underlying continuity between the two topics. We have

TABLE 7.3 Longitudinal Effects of Athletics on Delinquency for Whites in Sport-Oriented Small Towns (N = 161)

	Correlations (r) with Athletic Participation during High School					
	At Age 16		*At Age 18*		*At Age 24*	
Status Offenses						
School delinquency	–.17	(.01)	–.29	(.001)	–	–
Running away	+.08	(NS)	–.11	(.09)	–	–
Trouble with parents	–.04	(NS)	–.12	(.07)	–	–
Crime						
Index of serious delinquency	–.05	(NS)	–.18	(.01)	–.18	(.01)
Interpersonal aggression	–.10	(.09)	–.24	(.001)	–.13	(.05)
Theft and vandalism	–.05	(NS)	–.18	(.01)	–.20	(.005)

NOTE: NS = not significant.

found that religion, as an aspect of individual belief and behavior, has no restraining influence on deviance except as religion also gains living, active social expression. That is, in communities where only a minority belong to churches, even the most pious teenagers are no less prone to delinquency than are the least religious (Hirschi and Stark, 1969; Stark et al., 1981). Put another way, religion does not create conformity by its doctrines and rites, but only as it binds people to the moral order, to membership in the moral community. So described, religious effects are the property of social networks, not of individuals or even of religious activities such as Sunday school attendance. Religion restrains behavior where people lend it the power to do so.

Here we see that this also can occur with elements of wholly secular culture. As a purely personal attribute, participation in sports does not result in better behaved teenagers. Going daily to team practice, like going weekly to Sunday school, simply does not matter by itself. And, of course, for most white boys in this sample, sports were a personal activity unreinforced by community solidarity. But for blacks and for small town whites, sports participation is not a thing unto itself. Rather, it is the focus of intense community attention and interest. In this fashion, then, sports can be transformed into another means by which the power of moral communities can restrain, indeed, can reform. When sports are a focus of community solidarity they become invested with the capacity to reward athletes who conform to athletic ideals and to punish those who do not. As a colleague summed up our findings: "Shooting hoops does shape guys up, but only if enough people watch them shooting and really care."

8

Rational Choice and Determinism

JOHN S. GOLDKAMP

> We have moved forward by dispossessing autonomous man, but he has not departed gracefully. He is conducting a sort of rear-guard action in which, unfortunately, he can marshall formidable support [Skinner, 1978: 16].

RATIONAL CHOICE THEORY AND CLASSICAL THEMES

After a century of criminological research in the social sciences, much of which can be linked in method and substance to the positivist tradition, the free will versus determinism controversy concerning the nature of crime and criminal remains. Though some may view this debate as timeworn, overblown (see Gottfredson and Hirschi, this volume), or superficial in its current context, it was the issue over which the positivist school of criminology clashed most emphatically with classical criminological thought.

Many current policy questions, such as the constitutionality of preventive detention and the appropriateness of just deserts or selective incapacitation, are implicitly tied to assumptions about the nature of human actors, their freedom to choose their actions deliberately, and thus to the appropriateness of holding them responsible.

Rational choice theory, which views crime from the perspective of offender decision making, reintroduces the provocative themes of the rational, deliberative criminal of classical criminology (see, e.g., Piliavin et al., 1986; Cornish and Clarke, 1986; Clarke and Cornish, 1985; Becker, 1968). Clarke and Cornish's conceptualization of rational choice is eclectic. It summarizes elements of earlier economic models and elements of psychology and decision theory in three components:

"the image of a reasoning offender, a crime-specific focus, and the development of different decision models for involvement processes and the criminal event" (Cornish and Clarke, 1986).

The first element of their perspective, the "image of the reasoning offender," unabashedly posits a rational, calculating offender, capable of voluntary decisions and actions. They write that the "starting point" of the rational choice perspective

> was an assumption that offenders seek to benefit themselves by their criminal behavior; that this involves the making of decisions and of choices, however rudimentary on occasion these processes might be; and that these processes exhibit a measure of rationality, albeit constrained by limits of time and ability and the availability of relevant information [Cornish and Clarke, 1986: 1].

The crime-specific focus "was adopted, not only because different crimes meet different needs, but also because the situational context of decision making and the information being handled will vary greatly among offenses" (Cornish and Clarke, 1986: 2-3). The authors state clearly that the focus of their theoretical perspective "is on crimes rather than on offenders."

The third component distinguished between two kinds of offender decisions that have theoretical and policy relevance, broader decisions concerning overall "involvement" in crimes (beginning, continuing, and desisting), and narrower decisions to undertake specific crimes.

While this third component deals with the locus of rational decision making by the offender, the first two elements evoke the criminal of the classical school who weighs the costs and benefits of committing an illegal act before acting and who, if choosing crime and subsequently being caught, will receive punishment based on an assumption of responsibility. As Clarke and Cornish put it: "A criminology that makes use of such voluntaristic concepts might seem to have forsaken its traditional determinism." However, they are concerned less with the implications their framework has for the free will/determinism debate than with its heuristic value in integrating theory and research from a variety of disciplines and, one hopes, serving as a vehicle for informing crime control policy (Clarke and Cornish, 1985: 178).

Admittedly, this chapter focuses on an aspect of Clarke and Cornish's rational choice framework that the authors do not consider of central importance, given their larger aims. They explicitly set the free will question aside:

> We believe, then, that decision-making concepts can be used for the purpose of constructing "good enough" theories without necessarily being firmly committed to a particular position in the free will/determinism debate—or to any consequential implications for crime control . . . or criminal justice. . . . Indeed, the resulting policies remain, as before, neoclassical assumptions [Clarke and Cornish, 1985: 178].

This view coincides with the view of those who believe that a rehashing of the free will-determinism debate may not be a productive exercise. For example, Gottfredson and Hirschi (this volume) suggest that "criminologists, from Ferri to the present, overdraw the assumption of determinism." In fact, within a "positivistic" (i.e., deterministic) model, they contend that there is room for reasoning or voluntaristic processes to explain variation in criminal outcomes.

Without disagreeing with the goals of Clarke and Cornish's integrated rational choice framework or their characterization concerning the "uneasy blend" of assumptions that structure justice policy, this chapter takes advantage of the opportunity offered by their effort to reintroduce the rational criminal. I will reconsider the deterministic arguments of the classical school's nemeses, the early positivists, and weigh their viability today.

If the classical model of a reasoning criminal is viewed as a constructive organizing framework in current research, does the opposite position, the criminal of determinism, also have heuristic worth? Just how silly is the notion that the criminal is a product not a producer?

POSITIVISM AND CHOICE

Placed within the philosophical phraseology of his era (*On Crimes and Punishments* appeared in 1764)—during which Hobbes, Locke, then Rousseau, among others, elaborately debated the characteristics of "natural man" and the implications of his entry into "society"—Beccaria's use of the lawyer-like man who enters society through the social compact is not even slightly surprising. Beccaria's use of the intellectual imagery of his time in his work was not so much to add to that debate as it was to construct a platform for reform of the criminal justice system. Ferri praised Beccaria's contribution to fighting barbaric punishments and abuses of criminal procedure that were commonplace in the years prior to the French Revolution. But Ferri flatly rejected the assumption of classical criminology, giving man a "free will" that undergirded the extensive criminal law reform that had taken place in Europe (and moreover blamed the classical school for the mindless acceptance of prison as the sole coinage of criminal punishment).

In 1901, Ferri (1968: 60) lectured students at the University of Naples that

> the admission of a free will is out of the question. . . . Free will would imply that the human will, confronted by the choice of making voluntarily a certain determination, has the last decisive word under the pressure of circumstances contending for and against this decision; that it is free to decide for or against a certain course independently of internal and external circumstances, which play upon it, according to laws of cause and effect.

Although he was undeniably aware of Quetelet and Guerry, the French statisticians of the early nineteenth century, and the regularities in crime rates they discovered, Ferri traced the birth of positivist criminology to his senior Italian colleague, Lombroso. Lombroso's medical-anthropological research, classification of criminals, concept of the born criminal, and scientific method of analysis shifted emphasis from the crime to the criminal and to understanding why the criminal committed crime.

As Ferri pointed out at the turn of the century, and many others have since, a system of criminal punishment based on the notion that human beings are free to act and are responsible for their acts is wholly inappropriate if, in fact, they are not free to choose to act but rather are constrained toward or away from actions as a result of forces having little to do with choice. Not only did Ferri argue for a criminal jurisprudence based on what he considered these lessons of science but his research led him to move well beyond Lomroso's "scientific" classification of criminals and, more important, of causes.

Specifically, he moved beyond Lombroso's search for the born criminal and expanded theory concerning the ways in which human beings could be made criminal. He categorized causes of crime as "anthropological, telluric and social" claiming that "every crime from the smallest to the most atrocious, is the result of the interaction of these three causes" (Ferri, 1968: 76). Under the anthropological heading, Ferri included factors relating to the "organic and psychological" traits and personality of the offender, subsuming Lombroso's focus on anatomical characteristics, such as race, but extending broadly beyond into psychological influences. By "telluric" factors Ferri meant the "physical environment by which we live and to which we pay no attention" (Ferri, 1968: 81). By "social conditions," Ferri, early a Marxist but one who later accommodated to Italian fascism, was referring to economic and other aspects of social structure.

In expanding the scope of determinism in criminology, Ferri lay the groundwork for a variety of traditions following during the twentieth century. But at its core, nonetheless, Ferri's scientific criminology was based on rejection of the notion of the rational, autonomous actor key to the classical conceptualization. A man does not commit a crime because he wants to. According to Ferri (1968: 86, emphasis added):

> No, a man commits a crime because he finds himself in certain physical and social conditions, from which the evil plant of crime takes life and strength. Thus we obtain the origin of that *sad human figure* which is the product of the interaction of those factors, an abnormal man, a man not adopted to the conditions of the social environment in which he is born.... And the abnormal man who is below the minimum of adaptability to social life and bears the mark of organic degeneration develops either a passive or an aggressive form of abnormality and becomes a criminal.

SOCIAL AND PHYSICAL ENVIRONMENT: MODERN THEMES TO DETERMINISM

It is beyond the scope of this discussion to trace in detail the evolution of the varieties of social, environmental, and even biological determinist perspectives in criminology since the turn of the century. Once taboo, biological inquiries, for example, have recently become acceptable (Mednick, 1980), so that the long frustrated ghost of Lombroso must be smiling at last.

Brands of social determinism are legion. A striking turn of the century perspective, presaging later conflict theory, was Bonger's Marxist critique that rejected the Italian positivists strong leanings toward biological determinism in favor of a social-economic interpretation. In *Race and Crime* Bonger (1969: 105-107) argued that physical/psychological "predisposition is not predestination" and that "no person comes into the world a criminal." Instead, and he was as strongly disinclined to accept the free will man as was Ferri, he contended that "the cause [of crime] can only be found in the social environment, which is determined by the mode of production" (Bonger, 1969: 33). The modern social theories of crime that could be interpreted as deterministic are too numerous to be described here.

The psychological determinism referred to as a primitive science in the works of Ferri and Bonger was placed at center stage during much of the twentieth century thanks to the work of Freud, whose lusty and aggressive man was Hobbesian in his need to be controlled.

If Ferri's ghost has been made uncomfortable with aspects of psychoanalytically inspired interpretations of criminal behavior (Aichhorn, 1936; Redl and Winemann, 1951), it may have been encouraged by the development of social learning theory (Bandura, 1977) and might have been absolutely heartened by the work of Eysenck whose psychological approach to crime has clear biological underpinnings. In *Crime and Personality*, for example, Eysenck (1977: 195) appears to read directly from an Italian text:

> We would regard behavior from a completely deterministic point of view; that is to say, the individual's behavior is determined completely by his heredity and by environmental influences which have been brought to bear upon him.

Eysenck would not mince words in reacting to the mode of offender decision making proposed by rational choice theory. Eysenck (1977: 194) writes:

> It would be nice if human beings were rational beings, whose conduct was determined by the use of intelligence and guided by wisdom. However, the experimental evidence is now pretty conclusive that this picture of homo sapiens is unfortunately entirely false. Our conduct is guided much more by certain biological impulses which we share with the lower animals, and to disregard and neglect these facts is probably the most important reason for the sad state in which society finds itself today. Man is the most savage and deadly animal which has ever lived in the world, yet we fail to recognize the danger.

Nor has criminological research and theory neglected Ferri's "telluric" emphasis, if by this is meant both the influences of the physical environment and the physical-social environment of criminal behavior. From the ecological tradition of the Chicago School, the work of Burgess and Shaw and McKay, to the defensible space notions of Oscar Newman (see Baldwin, 1979, for a good review of this literature), it can be argued that the environment exerts a strong direct influence on the likelihood of crime (but see Taylor et al., 1984). In fact, one inference that may be drawn from the "situational" approach to crime prevention (see especially Clarke, 1983), which argues that by manipulating aspects of the physical environment crime levels and kinds may be influenced, is that the offender's actions are in part "determined" by the physical arrangement of his surroundings.

ENVIRONMENTAL DETERMINISM MORE BROADLY CONCEIVED: A BEHAVIORIST'S VIEW OF RATIONAL CHOICE

Clarke and Cornish (1985: 167-169) describe two arenas of offender decision making in organizing their rational choice framework concerning involvement in criminality (beginning, continuing, and desisting) and the specific criminal event. They argue that in becoming involved in crime, offenders must be found in a state of "readiness" or willingness to move in the direction of the criminal event. To arrive at these crossroads, a range of factors predisposing or inclining the offender to the possibility of criminal involvement may have great influence. These influences, such as psychological factors, upbringing, previous learning experiences, and general needs (among which the authors list "money, sex, friendship, status, and excitement") admittedly include many of the areas with which "traditional criminology has been preoccupied" (1985: 167-168).

But, just as Bonger may have said that "predisposition is not predestination," Clarke and Cornish (1985: 167) argue that such background factors are not directly criminogenic, but rather "they have an orienting function—exposing people to particular problems and particular opportunities and leading them to perceive and evaluate these in particular (criminal) ways." Thus "readiness" resembles a loose, standing decision such that "under the right circumstances (the criminal) would commit the offense" (1985: 167). Like recent decision theory, then, rational choice appears to provide a role for contextual variables, including personal factors affecting the decision maker that constrain the individual's decision-making abilities, but that do not as a result exclude a deliberate decision function (Hogarth, 1980).

Other contextual factors—aspects of the "task environment" (Hogarth, 1980)—become central in the decision making conducted by the offender in carrying out the criminal event. Once the offender decides to commit burglary, for example, Clarke and Cornish outline the kinds of information processing that the offender uses to arrive at the point of actually walking in the door of a residence. These may include ease of access to the dwelling, the frequency of police patrols, the absence of the residents, and so on (Clarke and Cornish, 1985: 169). Thus the act of burglarizing a particular house on a particular day at a particular time results from the offender's processing the relevant information and the weighing of the pros and cons. A role for specific deterrent approaches (situational measures) in addressing crime of this sort naturally follows in this rational schema: By altering the physical structure of dwellings, increasing police patrol, varying the resident's presence, and so on, the probability of apprehension (and, hence, of punishment) is dramatically increased and thus alters the rational offender's calculations of the risk and rewards involved.

Of course, it is just this classical, utilitarian conceptualization of the offender that Ferri, and his successors, have attempted to dispense with. At the same time, the "rational man" model continues to enjoy attention—not only in criminological theory but in criminal jurisprudence—there is a more radical determinist perspective, Skinner's science of behavior, which, though seldom applied in criminology, has relevance for the study and control of criminal behavior.

In analyzing the actions of human beings, Skinner (1978: 16-19) begins with a version of environmental determinism:

> In the traditional view, a person is free. He is autonomous in the sense that his behavior is uncaused. He can therefore be held responsible for what he does and justly punished if he offends. . . . A scientific analysis shifts the credit as well as the blame to the environment, and traditional practices can then no longer be justified.

In beginning his article, "Why I Am Not a Cognitive Psychologist," Skinner (1978: 97) states more directly that "the variables of which human behavior is a function lie in the environment." At this level, Skinner could be easily mistaken for Ferri or even Bonger in either's discussion of the role of the environment in determining individuals' actions.

But Skinner's determinism extends the reach of the environment beyond what the early criminologists might have conceived. Not only does he disavow the existence of freedom or its corollaries, autonomy and choice, he questions the existence of feeling, creativity, dignity, and *thinking* itself.

"Wanting is not a feeling," Skinner (1978: 35) writes, for example, "nor is a feeling the reason a person acts to get what he wants." Rather "certain contingencies" from the person's environment "have raised the probability of behavior and at the same time have created conditions which may be felt. Freedom is a matter of contingencies of reinforcement, not of the feelings the contingencies generate."

Thinking, which Skinner describes as the "last stronghold of the autonomous man," is also explained in terms of contingencies of reinforcement, though he notes that it has yielded slowly to explanation because of its complexity (1978: 184). Culture "promotes thinking by constructing special contingencies. It teaches the person to make fine discriminations by making differential reinforcement more precise. It teaches techniques to be used in solving problems. It provides rules that make it unnecessary to be exposed to the contingencies from which the rules are derived, and it provides rules for finding rules" (p. 185).

Not satisfied with denying humankind the vanity of thinking (and leaving us to contemplate the reverse of the Cartesian truth—I think, therefore I am), Skinner would appear to deprive man of "mind" and even of "consciousness": Mind he describes as an invention of the Greeks "to explain how the real world could be known" (1978: 104). Consciousness "is a social product. It is not only *not the special field of autonomous man, it is not within range of the solitary man" (p. 183). Consciousness for Skinner is a product of the (social) environment and has no meaning without it.*

Because for Skinner (1978: 189) the "self" then becomes merely "a repertoire of behavior appropriate to a given set of contingencies," behavior and goodness are matters mainly of control (one set of contingencies or another). "Goodness . . . waxes as visible control wanes, and so, of course, does freedom." An individual can be "good" only as long as there is freedom of choice to undertake good versus "bad" behavior. Because the environment controls the individual, "good" behavior cannot be good and criminal behavior cannot be bad. It is merely, in a complicated way, what the environment produces.

What of the implications of Skinner's science of behavior for rational choice theory or related conceptual frameworks? Not only would Skinner disagree with the assumption of rational decision making as voluntary choice undergirding the theoretical framework—as would many other determinists certainly—he would argue that even a limited role for choice making based on mentalistic processes is false and not supportable. What might look like thinking, such as the making of fine discriminations associated with involvement and criminal event decisions, is rather a response to contingencies of reinforcements generated by the environment. "When we do not know why people do one thing rather than another," he writes, "we say that they 'choose' or 'make decisions'" (1978: 102).

An intriguing implication of this perspective is that deterrence may work (or what looks like deterrence may work), but not because of Bentham's (1843: 402) formulation of human nature in which he postulated that

> in matters of importance everyone calculates. Each individual calculates with more or less correctness, according to the degrees of his information, and the power of the motives which actuate him, but they all calculate.

Rather, manipulation of contingencies of reinforcement (including aversive or punitive as well as reward-based influences)—such as situational measures—controls criminal behavior. Deterrence as a means of crime control, therefore, may be grounded in doses of pleasure and pain, but may have little to do with hedonistic calculus. Deterrence may just be another way of conjuring the Skinnerian mechanism of environmental control of behavior.

POSITIVISM'S LEGACY OF PESSIMISM

This chapter has reacted to the constructive notions of recent rational choice theory as a challenge to reconsider some of the substantive implications of the positivist-classical debate about free will versus determinism in understanding and controlling crime. Gottfredson and Hirschi have noted, in an earlier chapter, that questions springing from positivist methods of fact gathering and searching for correlates of criminal behavior should be separated from discussions of ideology or crime policy apparently flowing from the positivist tradition in criminology. They have rightly pointed out that the positivist's rejection of classical tenets in favor of positivism was an ideological act, not the result of scientific inquiry and conclusion, as should have been required by their perspective.

However, although it is not true that policy conclusions or political ideology associated with positivism necessarily stemmed from the birth of scientific method in the social sciences, it *is* true that determinism was a part of its substantive legacy. And questions concerning the nature of the human being and the criminal raised by these deterministic views remain unsettling and evoke a sense of pessimism about the future of dealing with crime (as well as with other human affairs).

This inference of pessimism derives from an impression that determinism strips individuals of responsibility for their acts, and as a result the framework of order buttressed by criminal law risks being a house of cards. Lombroso contributed his "born criminal," Ferri his "sad human figure," and Bonger his economic man driven by "cupidity." Freud offered man as a latent murderer and a sex offender, and Eysenck feared man as "the most savage and deadly animal who ever lived."

Yet the optimism that can be found in the texts of the determinists is based on a visionary belief in the perfectibility of humankind—through science, of course. Ferri, who would have redesigned the legal system based on his scientific approach (which would have abolished juries for experts and eliminated the concept of extenuating circumstances from the law, since all circumstances were extenuating), would have removed crime from society through "rules of preventive hygiene" based on science. (Punishment would have been abolished as irrelevant, though until all aberrant individuals were processed out of society, incapacitative uses of prison would temporarily remain.) Bonger would address the economic order and restore to man his natural "altruistic" nature, in line with the Marxist vision of a utopian society. Eysenck would identify criminals as children and through programs of conditioning train them to fit well into society without posing a danger.

Skinner's determinism would on the surface appear to contribute most to this sense of pessimism. If we do not "think," if we are the product of our environment rather than of our existential "selves"—and here the ghost of Sartre may be heard stirring—then how do we modify our behavior (warlike, criminal, or otherwise)? But this assumption that the message of behaviorism is profoundly pessimistic misunderstands the goals of science, according to Skinner. First, by destroying the myth of the autonomous man, Skinner (1978) argues, the science of behavior is performing a valuable service that will allow civilization to begin to move ahead on firmer footing:

> What is being abolished is autonomous man—the inner man, the homunculus, the possessing demon—autonomous man is a device used to explain what we cannot explain in any other way. He has been constructed from our ignorance, and as our understanding increases, the very stuff of which he is composed vanishes. Science does not dehumanize man, *it dehomunculizes him* [p. 191; emphasis added].

Having destroyed the autonomous man, the responsible man, what do the determinists offer in his place? Is the determined human being a chaotic being in need of control? If so, or even if only the determined criminal is in need of control, how can nonautonomous man manage himself? Are there some (Ferri's experts, Eysenck's staff who would test children to locate the likely future criminals?) whose fate it would be to manage the social order?

Skinner's response, and the key reason the science of behavior he outlines is an optimistic one according to him, is that although man may be controlled by his environment, "it is an environment almost wholly of his own making" (1978: 196). Thus on a grander scale than envisaged by Ferri perhaps, according to Skinner, man has the ability totally to redesign his environment and to construct "contingencies" that will eliminate problems such as war and crime that cannot be addressed if the myth of the autonomous man continues as the operating paradigm. Man has the ability to control himself.

In this regard, the implications for a behaviorist orientation to understanding crime might generate policies quite similar to what rational choice researchers might develop. Rather than modifying the environment through situational measures intended to increase the costs (the risks of being apprehended, and so on) to the calculating criminal as rational choice analysis might suggest, for example, the behaviorist might redesign the environment to manipulate the contingencies of reinforcement to eliminate the criminal behavior. The behaviorist engaged in constructing such a crime policy might ask why, if the resulting approach worked, it is necessary to give the potential offender properties (volition, autonomy) he or she does not have. The rational choice theorist designing a similar policy might ask why, even if the operation of the offender's "thinking" could not be proved (and if the policy worked), would it be harmful to assume that we can treat criminals (and other people) as if they were able to make decisions for which they could be held responsible.

To date it is fair to say that we can prove neither that humans operate in a rational mode nor that their behavior is mostly if not totally determined. In fact, when one considers the lack of resolution that has typified such debates historically—when one philosophical ideal (that of the rational human whom we may hold responsible) is argued over another (that of a utopian science of behavior holding the keys to the contingencies of the environment that control human behavior)—pragmatic approaches to crime may understandably have great appeal.

Thus Clarke and Cornish, who have set such questions aside in the interest of pragmatism, might ask, for example, how Skinner might approach the problem of gun control—now, not in some utopian future scenario. Or, despite the risks of treating a determined criminal as rational, they might argue the value of interviewing offenders to learn about how they perceive the crime event, how they assess targets, how they opt to proceed with specific crimes. Whether we view the criminal as functioning rationally or as being determined by environmental contingencies might be irrelevant—if, as a result, strategies can be developed to discourage criminal acts.

9

Supplementing the Positivistic Perspective

HANS TOCH

When I think about what I do as a social scientist, the experience evokes the parable of the blind men and the elephant, in that I know I must not reify reality fragments by forgetting where and how I acquired my data. Such is the essence of the positivistic tradition, which enjoins us to limit the role that faith can play in interpreting facts.

Positivism seeks to reduce subjectivity in scientific *inferences*. This is not the same as reducing *subjectivity as subject matter*, and a leap from the concern with how you look at something to a concern with what you are looking at is not a legitimate leap. Nevertheless, there are many who have made this leap in the past, and have suggested that positivists should avoid studying subjective data. In sociology the positivistic movement has thus highlighted a "tendency toward social structural explanations as distinct from those which refer to human interactions and motives" (Abercrombie et al., 1984: 164). A more drastic version of this same tendency appeared in psychology, where radical behaviorists rejected "mentalistic" data, considering them "unscientific." Talcott Parsons (1937: 117) concludes that this stance had become so embedded in the radical positivistic approach that "in the last analysis behavioristic objectivism is the only position for a radically consistent positivist to take." Parsons points out that the radical positivists sought to explain all behavior by describing its *antecedents*, by mapping the conditions under which the behavior occurs, so that "insofar as the 'conditions' ultimately form the sole determinants of action the subjective aspect becomes merely a reflection of these 'facts'; it is purely epiphenomenal" (p. 120). In this volume, Gottfredson and Hirschi tell us that the earliest positivists needed to fight battles that today's positivists no longer have to fight. One example of change is that "positivists [in criminology] now feel no need to obliterate the choice theories so passionately criticized by positivism's founders." Gottfredson and Hirschi also correctly suggest that there is no longer an "ineluctable connection to positivism" in the "assumption" that "criminal behavior can be explained without reference to the meaning that the behavior has for the criminal actor" (Greenberg, 1981: 2).

In this chapter I will argue that "the meaning that the behavior has for the criminal actor" is not only respectable data for a positivistic criminologist to seek and to obtain, but that such data are useful even where one favors the correlational methods discussed elsewhere in this volume. I have borrowed the title of my essay—and its theme—from a cursory history of criminological theory written for an undergraduate text (Toch, 1979). In this overview I noted:

> The questions that are left unanswered by early criminologists can be addressed if we go beyond the kind of data the positive school sought. . . . What we must specifically recognize in such supplementary research is that "a factor cannot become a cause before it is a motive" [B. Glueck, cit. Bovet, 1951].

My point relates to a juncture in the history of social science such as that Gottfredson and Hirschi describe. At its inception, positivism was concerned with rejecting animism and metaphysics as substitutes for scientific explanations (Aron, 1968: 76). Positivistic social scientists sought to emulate applied mathematicians, physicians, and other "hard" scientists in a direct approach to inferences. Given this aim, it made sense to reject "motives" as explanations of conduct because if you read motivation into a rock you are at best a primitive animist. Unfortunately, if you go further and conclude that mechanistic determinism (the scientific way to explain the movement of rocks) must be an encompassing scientific approach to *human* behavior you commit a reverse error. When we considered rocks-that-move, the danger was to read something into the phenomena under study; in the case of people, the danger is of omitting information that one cannot get about rocks, because as mechanical objects rocks are passive when they respond to impingements. Rocks are not repositories of separate variables, and if a rock could speak, one would learn nothing by asking it how it perceived a push or a shove and why it moved. Human subjects, however, react to impingements in different ways depending on how such impingements are perceived and interpreted, and how interpretations are reacted to in line with preexisting and emerging goals. Answers to criminological questions that are inferred from data about criminogenic impingements and offense behavior must therefore be verified and/or fleshed out through access to the human mind—that is, by communicating with offender-subjects. In the words of Allport (1962: 414),

> It is worth asking whether we ought to seek only objective validation for our measuring instruments. Why not demand likewise, where possible, subjective validation by asking our subject what he himself thinks of the dimensional diagnosis we have made. . . . Too often we fail to consult the richest of all sources of data; namely, the subject's own self-knowledge.

Allport implies that conceptual constructs, no matter how these are derived, should make sense (translated, if need be) to those who are the objects of theorizing. This may be an extreme requisite unacceptable to positivists, but a less ambitious and more achievable version of the ideal is Glueck's requirement, which would be that any construct that pretends to "explain" *human* behavior must tackle the question, What motivated the people I am studying to behave in the manner described? This means, among other things, that we must reconstruct the motives of individuals who give rise to aggregate behavior trends that are illuminated through correlations. The dictum rejects a version of human science that mimics nonhuman science by short-circuiting the human mind in efforts to explain human behavior. It requires a multimethod approach because it implies that inventories of independent variables (environmental antecedents) and dependent variables (behavioral consequences) and theories about human behavior become complete only through the study (including interviews) of the actors involved. Allport suggests a sequence for such multimethod approaches. He tells us (criminologists) that we not only can approach offenders as sources of hunches (which most of us think is respectable), but that person-centered inquiries can serve as correctives, checks, and criteria—in short, as supplements—to theories that are based on aggregate data. Allport (1962: 407) writes:

> For one thing we should ask, are our generalizations really relevant to the case we are studying? If so, do they need modification? And in what ways is this individual the asymptote of all our general laws? Or to state the procedure more simply: Why should we not start with individual behavior as a source of hunches (as we have in the past), but finally come back to the individual—not for the mechanical application of laws (as we do

> now), but for a fuller, supplementary, and more accurate assessment than we are now able to give?

The advent of this perspective in criminology is most easily traced to contributions of the Chicago School, and best reflected in detailed case histories of *The Jack Roller* (Shaw, 1930) and *Brothers in Crime* (Shaw, 1938). *The Jack Roller* was a book subtitled *A Delinquent Boy's Own Story*, and Shaw (1930: 17) wrote in the introduction "the 'own story' reveals the essentially human aspects of the problem of delinquency. For in such documents one gains a sympathetic appreciation of the child's own personal problems and the sort of world in which he lives." Faris (1979: 75-76), in his history of early Chicago sociology, reminds us that

> the investigators at the Institute for Juvenile Research and graduate students at the University of Chicago gathered (delinquent life history) cases by the thousands. Shaw's customary procedure in getting a life history was to persuade a boy in a correctional institution to write it for him . . . promising him that it would be used for research purposes only. In a typical case a boy would first write only a brief account of his whole life. Shaw would then have it expanded by pointing to a particular section, remarking that it interested him, and asking for more details on that part. This procedure was repeated for other sections, and sometimes for parts within an expanded section.

Faris (1979) quotes Burgess as stressing that Shaw's case studies brought "realism to criminology." Burgess speculated that "empirical American sociology was perhaps popularized and transmitted to all corners of the world by the Shaw monographs more than by any other examples of this brand of sociological research" (Faris, 1979: 76).

The delinquent Stanley, the protagonist of *The Jack Roller*, kept a diary for research purposes. He was repeatedly interviewed by Clifford Shaw, who was a proficient stenographer. Stanley was also examined by the psychiatrist William Healy, who worked as a consultant with Shaw and McKay and their colleagues. Healy, in conjunction with Augusta Bronner, later embarked on a four-year (1929-1933) case-oriented research project, the results of which are reported in *New Light on Delinquency and Its Treatment* (Healy and Bronner, 1969). Healy and Bronner's book is, in my estimation, an enduring classic that has contemporary relevance and import because Healy and Bronner provide one of the more convincing examples we have available of a "positivistic" (data-based) deployment of information derived from interviews. The link may justify reviewing what Healy and Bronner attempted to do, and what inferences they drew from their findings.

Healy and Bronner collected in-depth material about 153 serious delinquents, 145 nondelinquent siblings, and 133 families from which the delinquent and control subjects derived. In total, 105 delinquents were paired with control siblings close to them in age. These pairs included eight sets of twins involving one delinquent and one nondelinquent twin. The point of mentioning the numbers is to show that Healy and Bronner's study—despite its case-focus—included respectable Ns and defensible criteria for the selection of its subjects. Though Healy and Bronner (1969: 17) tell us that "the research was not undertaken with the purpose of accumulating statistics concerning delinquency, and we insist that our findings have no large statistical values, aside from the purposive omission of mental defectives, the cases taken are representative of the potentially serious offenders that appear before a juvenile court in American urban communities" and that "on the whole we must conclude that we have a fair sampling of the repeatedly delinquent, of the families from which such delinquents spring, and of the conditioning factors which make for delinquency." The reference in this quote to "conditioning factors"—to poverty, unemployment, broken homes, and deteriorated neighborhood conditions—shows Healy and Bronner's healthy respect for positivistic criminological schemes that were current during the period in which their study was conducted.

Healy and Bronner's study, I submit, was a clear corrective to radical positivism in that it includes research strategies that were innovative and different from either simplistic or promiscuous data collection procedures. One such difference is the fact the Healy and Bronner simultaneously posed the questions, "Why does a delinquent gravitate toward delinquency? How does the nondelinquent escape becoming a delinquent? How can the same environment (or ostensibly the same environment) produce the delinquent and the nondelinquent?" Of these questions, the first acquires special and different connotations when it is paired with the second and subsumed under the third. Of the three questions, it is the second that was most unusual and held the greatest fascination for Healy and Bronner (1969: 23), who wrote that "no line of inquiry concerning causations seemed likely to be more fruitful than the key question: Why has a comparable sibling in the same family not been a delinquent?" Elsewhere, Healy and Bronner ruminated that

> if so many of the circumstances and attitudes revealed by these studies of family life are deleterious and provocative of delinquency—and who can

> doubt that they are active influences—the wonder is that no more of the siblings are delinquent. . . . And so why not study the nondelinquent for the purpose of discovering how he escaped being an offender [p. 24]!

In collecting data, almost equal attention was given to fleshing out the case histories of delinquents and nondelinquents. The chronologies included the problems each child presented to the families, and the problems the families presented to the delinquent and nondelinquent siblings. Among data collected by Healy and Bronner, no facts are more revealing than those related to evolving parent-child transactions for delinquents and nondelinquents. The methodology was uniquely equipped to explore these differences because only comparisons that included inventories of behaviors, feelings, and attitudes could have yielded discriminations, such as the discovery that for each set of parents there were

> great differences in their feelings and behavior toward their different children—more sympathetic understanding, more fulfillment of fundamental needs, less inconsistent treatment very frequently indeed having been exhibited from early years toward one child as compared to the other [1969: 9].

Completing the picture required tracking the children's reaction, which yielded findings such as the following:

> It finally appears that no less the 91 *percent of the delinquents* gave clear evidence of being or having been very unhappy and discontented in their life circumstances or extremely disturbed because of emotion-provoking situations or experiences. In great contradiction we found similar evidences of inner stress at the most in only *13 percent of the controls* [1969: 122].

Details in case materials permitted Healy and Bronner to describe and to explain diverging parent-child relationships. Cues had appeared in aggregate data that included sizable differences in characteristics that could (in infancy) start some children off at a disadvantage with more susceptible parents. For instance,

> great *restlessness* or *overactivity* was frequently reported by parents, teachers, and others to be an habitual characteristic of the delinquent; in not a few cases it was observed by members of our staff. . . . In this category, and we repeat that we are enumerating merely those who

> showed this behavior to a most unusual or abnormal degree, we found one third of our total number of delinquents, 53 cases. We are forced to agree with some other students of behavior problems that hyperactivity on the part of children is strongly related to the appearance of delinquency. In our series no single personality characteristic is found in any exaggerated degree so frequently [1969: 44-45].

Differences between future delinquents and nondelinquents of the sort that could stimulate adverse parental reactions were recorded at birth—for prenatal conditions and early postnatal development. In total, 74 developmental defects of this sort appeared for control siblings, compared to 170 for future delinquents. These and other differences involved potentially irritating attributes that could spark parental sequences of rejection.

The virtue of Healy and Bronner's case material is that it documents the ways in which child attributes and parental attitudes can intersect to produce family experiences almost calculated to occasion frustration and resentment among incipient delinquents. Healy and Bronner provide illustration after illustration that shows the importance of interviews in illuminating degenerating sequences. For example, in the case of one pair of twins,

> An amazing difference of attitude on the part of the father toward the delinquent and the control was reported to us and acknowledged by him. He maintained that the cause of it was the stubborn lack of response to him shown by the delinquent when an infant, only two months old. He said he detested the boy and had ever since—"I can't bear to have him touch me. I would rather have a snake around me than have him." Though the mother stated that the father always repulsed the boy when the latter attempted to climb on his knee, both parents insisted that the child had never given expression to any strong feelings about being disliked by his father [1969: 96].

The predelinquent boy's stoic exterior—which the father cited as "a stubborn lack of response"—hid a keen sense of awareness of hurt and evolving resentment, which the boy himself described in detail during interviews:

> He went on to give in the plainest language the vile epithets which his father called him and also the equally opprobrious terms that his parents applied to each other. He showed much feeling about all this, saying that he was going to hit his father "right on the chin" someday. . . . The control,

> he said, never did such things. It came out very clearly that the boy felt extremely insecure in his family relationships and that he greatly craved recognition and affection [1969: 97].

By contrast, the nondelinquent sibling (a twin) in the same family

> was very sure of himself and quite well satisfied with things as they were. In speaking of his brother to the psychologist he priggishly boasted, "I am the good boy" [1969: 97].

Healy and Bronner not only interviewed all the parents and children, but also spoke to teachers, relatives, and uninvolved siblings who could shed light on the interpersonal transactions involving the subjects and their families. In one case of twins:

> The sisters gave a clear account of the close relationship that had existed between his mother and the control; he followed her about and did household tasks with her. Generally the delinquent was not in the house long enough to do anything. As they grew older the control was very confidential with the mother and after she died was chummy with his sisters. The delinquent was always reticent with his family and sometimes sat about as if he had something on his mind. The father, a very restless man, "crabby and grouchy," seemed to dislike the delinquent from his early years; the sisters stated that this probably was because the boy was so much like himself. He always preferred the control who was of smiling and placid disposition, much like the mother in this respect.
>
> The father frequently whipped the delinquent as he had done some of his other children but was much more tender with the control. It was the sisters' opinion that though the delinquent was not nearly so demonstrative and cried little after his mother's death, in reality he felt her loss even more keenly than did his twin [1969: 114].

A review of Healy and Bronner's illustrative materials shows different and sometimes contrasting links between child attributes and parental reactions, such that a given trait could lead to rejection in one home and would promote acceptance or cement relationships in another. A physically active extrovert would thus tax one set of parents, but a similarly constituted boy could be prized (and favored) by a machismo-oriented father. A child's precocity could prevent parental bonding in one home and a child's retardation in another. Sibling coalitions sometimes aggravated and sometimes ameliorated rejection;

so did school placement or teacher attitudes. One delinquent, for example,

> maintained that a teacher in reading had made fun of him and told the other pupils that he was a "dumb bell"—"she never did like me." He didn't know how to dance and didn't want to and he insisted that another teacher smacked his face because he said so. He was put in an ungraded school after the first three years and hated that. His whole school career after those first years had been most unfortunate—while his brother was getting along well. He developed much fantasy life about being on a ship or being a forest ranger. Then after his gang contacts he began daydreaming about being a gangster in Chicago, having a big car, and robbing stores and banks with machine guns. "I would imagine I would get away with the money and buy a yacht and an aeroplane" [1969: 119].

This boy's sibling had fewer skills and aptitudes, but enjoyed acceptance (which he reciprocated) in school.

The thrust of Healy and Bronner's documentation relates to evolving predispositions toward prosocial or deviant behavior that are derived from satisfactory or unsatisfactory links with significant others. The point of stressing such links was to show that the negative variables conventionally highlighted by macrosociological theory did not directly, in themselves, produce delinquency—that among nondelinquents their impact was neutralized by warm and/or supportive relationships. To promote delinquency, criminogenic contextual forces must reinforce adverse relationships between parent and children. And even

> when either father or mother seems to be an outstandingly unfortunate influence, sometimes the other parent has appeared to have been much more potent in forming the character of a given child . . . almost all of the presumably inimical factors in family life can be and sometimes are negligible for the development of character, if some one positive constructive relationship influences the growing child. On the other hand, some single destructive relationship may be enough to turn the tide of conduct tendencies in the wrong direction [1969: 33].

As for the motives that lead to delinquency, Healy and Bronner (just as most sociologists) characterize these motives as "rational." They use the term to suggest that *given* an emotional vacuum or denigrating cumulative feedback experienced during formative years, a predelinquent learns that the prosocial world is not an arena for the satisfaction of needs and he or she searches for alternative arenas. Delinquency ultimately "makes sense" because it seems to offer compensatory relationships, and provides substitute routes to achieving purposefulness, acceptance, and indices of esteem:

> Through careful analysis of our accumulated data concerning delinquents and their families it became more and more clear that the delinquent's behavior had a very specific meaningfulness for the offender himself. It grew obvious that delinquency as a reactive response represented an attempted solution of the individual's problem; it seemed to promise certain satisfactions; it was a way out of the often blindly felt states of dissatisfaction [1969: 202].

My aim in reviewing some of Healy and Bronner's book is not to resuscitate history but to highlight what is possible. Healy and Bronner showed us that clinical (person-centered) inquiry is compatible with good research designs and with a sample combining respectable numbers and demonstrated representativeness. If we claim (as I do) the desirability of supplementing macrosociological approaches with interview-based studies, the criterion of representativeness—which psychiatric case studies have customarily ignored—is a key requisite.

Healy and Bronner included in their own data base the demographic variables recorded by sociologists of their day. They located delinquents and nondelinquents along parameters, mapping their larger environment, and they showed that criminogenic factors described in aggregate studies were operative. Since we know *who* Healy and Bronner's subjects are, communication with macrosociologists is possible in addressing process questions (the "how?" of delinquency theory) and when we ask the motivation-related questions ("why?") that require person-centered data.

Divergence occurs elsewhere. Unlike the sociologists of their day (but just as control theorists today), Healy and Bronner compared delinquents subjected to criminogenic variables to nondelinquents who were exposed to the *same* variables. As a consequence, positivistic theory (at least the orthodox or stripped down version of such theory) applies *only* to some of Healy and Bronner's subjects (the predelinquents) but not to the others (the nondelinquents). Healy and Bronner overlap with positivistic views in tracing delinquency where criminogenic variables are present and the dynamics that are inferred illuminate the probabilities highlighted by statistics. Where the overlap is absent (in the tracing of nondelinquency where standard criminogenic variables are present),

Healy and Bronner transcend most criminology—especially of their day. Clifford Shaw's case studies had answered the question, "How is delinquency learned?" and Shaw had anticipated the question, "*Why* is delinquency learned given favorable conditions?" A complete answer to the problem of delinquency causation, however, is possible only where we can ask with Healy and Bronner, "Why is delinquency *not* learned where conditions are favorable?" and this leaves "Why (and how) is delinquency learned where conditions are *not* favorable?"—to complete the picture that is required for comprehensive theorizing.

Healy and Bronner invoked relationship-centered variables rather than person-centered variables to "explain" delinquency. This fact matters because person-centered variables are variables that can be mechanistically invoked, and can produce indiscriminate catalogues that say as little about personal motivation as do their sociological counterparts. Such was the fate of Lombroso's theory and (curiously enough) that of Healy's (1915) himself.

Healy and Bronner's version of delinquency causation would today be classed (following Dewey and Bentley, 1949) as a "transactional" perspective. Transactional views link the person and the environment by explaining one as a product of the other, so that neither is a constant that can be independently specified. Interpersonal bonds (of parents and nondelinquents) and counterpart bonding failures (for parents and predelinquents) hinge on person-centered attributes that give them their shape. Predelinquent and nondelinquent "traits" have meaning only through the role they play as stimuli, cementing or undermining interpersonal links between children and their evolving world.

This perspective is ecumenical, in that it interfaces between generic theories and idiographic or clinical approaches. The fact has become evident with the ascendance of control theory (Hirschi, 1969), whose emphasis on the causal role of personal attachment validates Healy and Bronner and is validated by Healy and Bronner. Healy and Bronner's case studies in retrospect flesh out Hirschi's inferences about the role of attachment and go beyond these inferences by showing how attachment or failures of attachment evolve in each family.

Supplementary clinical research in this area could take many forms. It could extend Healy and Bronner's scheme by focusing on the later stages of the sequence, emphasizing positive (delinquency-oriented) motives that spring from negative (growing away from prosocial institutions) dispositions. Research could explore different or alternative responses to bonding failure, such as various forms of mental disease or involvements in family violence. Research of this kind is potentially critical because it may link criminology to areas such as mental health and lead to more comprehensive theories of human motivation.

INTERFACE ISSUES

Healy and Bronner offer a promise of interdisciplinary confluence, but the quality of their work (and the hospitality of control theory to an interdisciplinary perspective) makes the enterprise look easier than it has proven in practice. Difficulties arise where positivistic theories have shown disdain for motivational issues—and/or for process concerns in general—or where generic motives are arbitrarily ascribed to population subgroups. No links are forged where blind empiricism is deployed in the specification of objectively defined variables and where clinicians are precluded from translating such variables into motives. A good example is Monahan's (1981) volume on violence prediction, which is subtitled *An Assessment of Clinical Techniques,* but contains no provision for the exploration of violence-related motives through clinical interviews or psychometric instruments.

Supplementation of positivism requires the sort of closure that includes *both* the specification of reliable variables (traits and/or conditions) and the inquiry into how these variables impinge on individuals and translate into personal motivation. Probabilities and correlations must be set aside so that process questions can be explored. In the case of prediction (which is Monahan's concern) we must thus approach the individual case—as Allport points out—de novo. Allport (1962: 411-412) writes as follows:

> Suppose we take John, a lad of 12 years, and suppose his family background is poor; his father was a criminal; his mother rejected him; his neighborhood is marginal. Suppose that 70 percent of the boys having similar background become criminals. Does this mean that John himself has a 70 percent chance of delinquency? Not at all. John is a unique being, with a genetic inheritance all his own; his life-experience is his own. His unique world contains influences unknown to the statistician; perhaps an affectionate relation with a certain teacher, or a wise word once spoken by a neighbor. Such factors may be decisive and may offset all average probabilities. There is no 70 percent chance about John. He either will or will not become delinquent. Only a complete understanding of his personality, of his present and future circumstances, will give us a basis for sure prediction.

What Allport does not mention but could have mentioned is that a truly representative sample of a 70% risk group would produce (if valid) a set of individual cases, 70% of which would be 100% positive and 30% would be 100% negative. In each of these cases, clinical "understanding" would help us to try to ascertain the person's violence-prone versus nonviolence-prone subgroup membership, and (more important) could tell us *why* the case is either a likely positive or negative case and *how* the most relevant motives evolved. This information can then help us to group cases meaningfully in terms of motives and permits us to "explain" (understand the role of) standard predictors (such as gender, age, and ethnicity) that are otherwise blindly and atheoretically invoked. It is this process that Glueck referred to that ultimately converts a "factor" into a "motive" to produce a "cause." It is this process that also ultimately supplements "positivism" to produce full-bodied, comprehensive "positive" theories—theories that can link types of perspectives to enhance the understanding of human behavior.

ASSUMPTIONS, INTERVIEWS, AND INFERENCES

To subserve science, interviews of subjects must have focus, and case materials must be informed by theory, or at least, by selective perception. We know that "case workups" have always proved sterile. By providing us too many facts, they diffused our attention rather than guiding it. Histories of offenders yielded rosters of criminogenic variables that varied in contribution to outcome, and included noncriminogenic variables that appeared criminogenic when we employed *ex post facto* reasoning. We cannot explain behavior by hunting for favorite antecedents or by putting words in the mouths of informants.

The Healy-Bronner approach bears on these points. Their research admittedly featured overkill, since Healy belonged to the "every-fact-may-be-important" school of clinicians. But two features of their approach ensured against sterility: (1) offender-nonoffender comparisons permitted the discarding of hypothetically criminogenic antecedents that did not discriminate (e.g., socializing influences shared by the groups) and (2) a key variable—that of the parent-child transaction—combined open-endedness of inquiry—to avoid contamination of data—with specificity of focus.

The issue of focus is one that strikes me as the key issue. In our own explorations of the problem of violence chronicity (e.g., Toch, 1980) we have obtained offenders' versions of their violent behavior. We circumscribed offender accounts by (1) limiting our inquiry to interactions (incidents) culminating in violent behavior, (2) chronologically mapping the interpersonal "moves" of violence participants, and (3) exploring perceptions, assumptions, and feelings that pertained to each step in the chronology of interactions.

The approach illustrates linkages between (1) assumptions about causal variables, (2) the focus of clinical inquiry, and (3) deployment of data to inform theory. Offense behavior—the repeated deployment of physical violence—was regarded as a product (in unknown proportions) of personality-related dispositions and of social impingements that mobilized these dispositions. The interview was designed to explore the variabilities and consistencies of interpersonal situations and of reactions to them. The process yielded portraits of consistency in individual offender reactions across situations, and of variations in patterned reactions of violent offender subgroups.

A typology of this kind intersects with other data sources and explanatory schemes, because (among other things) it enables us to (1) trace violence-prone dispositions to socialization experiences that produce them; (2) correlate violence-related dispositions to different personality attributes; (3) inquire into differential group membership of types; and (4) venture predictions that feature the person in the situation.

A different sort of example is that of a prison study (Toch, 1977) based on assumptions central to environmental psychology (Ittleson et al., 1974). The premises have to do with congruities and incongruities between persons who inhabit environments (in this case, convicted offenders) and the environments they inhabit (in this case, prisons). Interviews were designed to elicit features of prison life that mattered to inmates. The interview included, among other things, a "self anchoring scale" (Cantril, 1965) that we adapted for prison use. This procedure permits respondents to imagine "best possible" and "worst possible" environments, and to rate real settings against self-defined anchors.

The interview yielded reliable dimensions of significant environmental requisites and they suggested variations in hierarchies of preferences that were correlated with (among other things) background variables such as age, institutional experiences, and subculture background. Interview-based dimensions yielded item pools, which evolved into a forced choice "prison preference" inventory. We administered this instrument to larger samples of inmates, to provide a quantifiable basis for a study of commonalties and differences in reactions to prison settings (Toch, 1977).

The point of mentioning this experience is to illustrate another connotation of "focus" and a different sort of link between clinical and nonclinical data. The sequence in this case moves from a theory that predicts differentiation to interview-derived variables in instrumented surveys. These surveys permit further extensions, such as "objective" inventories of prison attributes, behavioral consequences of "matches" and "mismatches" between people and settings, and inquiry into antecedents and personality correlates of different environment-centered needs (Wright, 1985).

The view I am defending implies that criminology can benefit by illuminating the "black box" (offender perspectives) that intervenes between conventional independent variables (criminogenic influences) and dependent variables (antisocial behavior). I believe that such benefits accrue, however, only if information can be accommodated by its consumers. For example, learning models—such as conditioning or differential association views—do not make the necessary accommodation. The hospitality to clinically derived data may have different origins, but premises that may help include the assumptions that:

(1) Macrovariables (such as level of unemployment or rate of criminality), among other things, are summaries of individual fates (such as persons being unemployed or unemployable, and offenders offending) and that in this way variables can be viewed as exercising influence at the individual level (being unemployed can enter into criminogenic motivation) or be influenced at that level (ditto).
(2) Social reality is always constructed by the perceiving person and is never completely defined by inventorying circumstances that impinge on actors.
(3) Societal or group interpersonal influence is interactive, and it must accommodate contributions of those who are influenced.
(4) Admittedly, personality can be treated as a variation on social themes, but this does not mean it is discardable as "noise" in one's equation.
(5) Phenotypically different behavior can be similarly motivated, and similar behavior can be differently motivated.
(6) Similar personal experiences can produce different behavioral outcomes, and different experiences can have similar outcomes.

The contention is that such premises enable. If they are accepted, one implied referent of theory becomes the offender, whose integrity can be preserved or violated in aggregate schemes, depending on whether we accommodate offender-relevant constructs such as those I have cited.

In what I have said I may have extended what Glueck meant by "motive," but the point he made that I have here strongly endorsed is that content-of-mind matters. The research that explores such content is "clinical." This means that persons are approached without being precategorized, pregrouped, or premerged and are subject to interviews. I have suggested that "clinical" does not imply aimless, anything-goes exploration, and that "clinical" also does not imply disrespect for representativeness or unconcern with reliability or contempt for non-clinically derived data.

Given the extension of clinical approaches to criminologically relevant issues, I am suggesting that links between clinically oriented investigators and some investigators reared in other traditions can be forged.

Theory would be impoverished if the clinician's scientific interest is largely unreciprocated. Such was the fate of Healy and Bronner, due to the dominance of early positivist thinking in their day. It is my hope—and the point of this chapter—that contemporary criminology could become more hospitable, given the advent of "softer," more sophisticated and more interdisciplinary theoretical perspectives.

10

Making Criminology Policy Relevant?

LESLIE T. WILKINS

Fashion is important in all forms of human activity, including social research. Recently there has been a demand for crime research to be "policy relevant." That is not to say that there has been a call for policy relevant research—the idea of policy relevance is a constraint upon, rather than a stimulus to, research studies. The implications of this trend are of importance to the design of social research, as well as to the interpersonal relationships between those who have come to see themselves either as "customers for" or "producers of" such research studies. In this chapter, we will examine a few of the consequences of the recent emphasis on "relevance" as it may affect both management styles and the quality of the findings of social research in the area that has become known as "criminology."

IS POLICY RELEVANT, RESEARCH RELEVANT?

What is the cause of crime? What, in any case, is "crime?" Which kind of treatment, punishment, or other action taken about offenders will reduce crime and recidivism? On what grounds is punishment justified? Is criminal activity associated with intelligence? What, in any case, is "intelligence"? Which, if any, of these questions qualify as "policy relevant"? Which, if any, are appropriately phrased research questions? Who decided this?

It is interesting to note that the question, "What is crime?" is regarded as a serious question in only most limited circles. The layperson has no difficulty at all in recognizing a crime when he or she sees one. And if, by chance, the act is not so defined in law, most people believe, there is no doubt that all right-minded persons would say that it "ought to be a crime."

But is this a serious viewpoint? Is "crime" something that is instantly recognized by all reasonable people? Many philosophers of the past have taken this view and there is contemporary support also in the writings of the Oxford legal philosopher, Hyman Gross (1979). In *A Theory of Criminal Justice* he asserts, "No one needs to refer to law books to know that murder is a crime." Of course, he does not claim that all regulations that have attached to them some form of penal sanction are to be instantly recognized by all citizens, though the law of many countries seems to work on this supposition. Rather it is claimed that there are a number of serious offenses that, everywhere (or everywhere that matters!), are known to be "crimes." This classification is a version of the division of crimes and offenses into two categories that was, and with some still is, a popular taxonomy in jurisprudence; namely, the division into crimes that are *mala in se* (wrong in their own right) and *mala prohibita* (wrong because so declared by statute). The Baroness Wootton (1959) dismissed this classification with contempt, equating *mala in se* with *mala antiqua.*

If there is no satisfactory definition of the field of inquiry—if there is no agreement as to "what is" crime, we must expect a considerable number of difficulties when we seek to select appropriate methods to study whatever we think it is. If there are problems with the identification of individual cases, aggregation will not provide a basis for analysis. But there are data that are recognized as "crime statistics." Is this not an acceptable basic count of identified "criminal acts?" Of course, it is accepted by those who would grant standing to these data that there is a "dark figure" of undetected crimes. But it seems usually to be assumed that the "dark figure" is of the same kind as the figures that are not "dark." Various attempts have been made to discover more about the "dark figures" of crimes. Presumably, all such attempts have as a common belief the utility of some construct of "crime." In other words, some definition is developed out of the operational constraints of the methods of investigation. But crime, from the earliest records, has been associated more with drama than with rational inquiry. Perhaps even the term *crime* is emotionally charged and, for that reason, an unsuitable concept upon which to base reasoned analysis?

WHOSE LANGUAGE?

Is this introductory discussion trivial? Does it matter precisely how crime is defined? Surely there is a large body of agreement and there is no point in wasting time. The public—those who pay for social research—do not approve of the in-fighting over jargon, they want answers to the problem of crime. What, demands the taxpayer, are these criminologists doing about crime? The current conclusion seems to be that they are doing little of significance and that what is being done is not desirable in the public cause. There follows, therefore, a demand for more severe punishment and for action that the layperson "understands." Few current policies seem to owe anything to research studies in the past, and hence in the future if research is to be tolerated, it must be "policy relevant."

There are doubtless many reasons for the fact the results of social research are seldom directly utilized in social policy decisions. If anything is to be done about "crime" as the public see it, then the definition used by the layperson must be used as the basis for inquiry. If any other definition of crime is used, then whatever is being dealt with is not (by definition!) crime as defined by the public. Thus perhaps we should hope that there is some point in Gross's claim that the laypersons' definition is correct and there is no need to refer to law books, provided one concentrates on the serious crimes. Perhaps little social research is utilized in social policy decisions, because, quite appropriately, there is reluctance to put into effect answers that address the wrong questions!

In this chapter we hope to work through to a reconciliation of these seemingly opposing perspectives. We will take note of the differences of viewpoints of those who prefer research activity and those who are concerned with social action. We will also consider a general, indeed classical, problem of research design that may afford a partial explanation of the difficulties. In the last part we will put forward some suggestions for "policy relevant" research.

STATEMENTS OF QUESTIONS

The importance of identification of appropriate questions has been recognized from the seventeenth century. It was reported by a certain John Aubrey that "Dr. Pell was wont to say that in the Solution of Questions, the Main Matter was the well-stating of them: which requires mother-wit and logic . . . for let the Question be well-stated, it will work almost of itself." Perhaps many social research workers have not yet taken the challenge of "logic" and "mother-wit"! It is, of course, easy to acknowledge the truth of Dr. Pell's claim, but the injunction to use mother-wit and logic does not provide much by way of instruction as to the appropriate form of questions—particularly questions that are intended to serve as the reference for research design.

It is worthwhile to distinguish two classes of problem relating to whether issues are or are not properly addressed by research methods. In this chapter I shall consider only one. I will not consider whether the issues that it is proposed to investigate are proper issues for investigation, that is to say, we will not discuss the moral concerns some people may have regarding the application of research methods in certain areas of human interest. I shall discuss only the form, style, and relevance of the research questions in themselves. That is, we will consider whether the research questions, as usually formulated, may be at fault and hence a common reason for the lack of successful applications of answers derived by social research, and specifically, criminological research techniques.

PERCEPTION OF PUBLIC INTEREST

Merton (1938) discussed, and Snow used in his novel, the idea of conflicting cultures of research and administration, particularly in government work. Certainly, it seems, the two classes of occupations are rewarded for kinds of performance that are not concordant with each other. Administrators are rewarded if they are able to anticipate trouble and to deal with it before it disturbs those who pay them. Thus administrators do not like to be surprised—clearly they should not have been surprised if they were "on top of their job." Scientists, on the other hand, find surprise exciting and often rewarding. Indeed, it has been suggested that a most important indicator of the value of scientific work is the degree of surprise it occasions among the members of related disciplines. Administrators will see themselves as "responsible" for decisions—they cannot get away with merely giving advice or providing estimates of probabilities. They have to choose between alternatives. They may "commission" the research worker to identify the available alternatives and to advise on them, but the final selection falls upon him or her, and if it is not right, administrators, not scientists, are the ones who will get the blame. Thus government officials come to see themselves as "customers" for social research; free to purchase if it seems worth the money, and free to ignore the results even though they were paid for.

The conflicting cultures of research and administration can, perhaps, be accommodated by a variety of arrangement methods. But it is more significant to our discussion at this stage to note that research workers and government policymakers are liable to interpret differently a most important concept that is central to both their roles, namely, the concept of the public interest. This may arise in part from the perception of "customer" and "client" roles, which leads to the idea of research as providing a kind of "product." The need, in turn, to see the required research outcome as a form of "product" arises from the belief that research workers are liable to disturb the environment because they are unable to appreciate all the political considerations that must be taken into account by the administrator. In commercial and industrial applications of social research, the position is somewhat different from that in government agencies. But, if we ignore the provision of security systems, little crime research falls into the private sector. The linkage between the public and the private sector is through the flow of money, whereas in democracies, the connection between the public and the government sector is through the ballot box and the concept of "public opinion." In the interpretation of the link between public opinion and public interest, and between public interest and public policy, the two cultures will be unlikely to have complete agreement.

CRIMINOLOGY: PUBLIC IMAGE AND IMAGINATION

If the final "product" of criminological research is to have any public policy significance, it is relevant to ask what "criminology" is. More simply, since criminologists "do" criminology, we might ask what do criminologists do? What would criminologists claim to do, and how does this compare with the image the public has of what is done, or should be done? It may be true, to a greater or lesser degree, of all forms of social research, but in the field of criminology it is obvious that what is being done is specifically not in accord with public opinion. In fact, it is just those issues that, as the public sees them, do not need to be investigated that criminal justice research workers seem to think most call for study. Everyone knows—everyone, that is, who has made no study of the matter—that the death penalty deters and reduces the risk of death at the hands of murderers. Everyone knows—except those who have research reports—that the use of "soft drugs" leads directly to the use of "hard drugs." It is "self-evident" that the longer the sentence, the greater the deterrence value of it to others who might consider such kinds of crime, and the less likely it is that the individual offender will recidivate. Myths of this kind could be multiplied to cover the field. So the public asks why money should be spent by these social scientists on investigations of that which is patently obvious to any thinking person. The relationship between public interest and public opinion is not a simple one, and not within the scope of this chapter. Nonetheless, it must be recognized that problems in social research may frequently arise because of the disjunction between the public image of research, general public opinion, and the commonly accepted views of public interest.

Scientific questions must, it seems, normally be structured in a different form from the questions posed by the general public. There may well arise, from this necessity, a difficulty of fitting research strategies to social policy in accord with the manner in which administrators interpret the relationship between public opinion and public interest. To the administrator, an unconditional acknowledgement of public opinion may sway the interpretation of public interest. The social scientist is no less concerned with the public interest, and often equally aware of public opinion, but is likely to see a greater divergence between these concepts.

A RULE FOR QUESTION FORM

We must set aside for a while, further consideration of the public interest in social research and take note of some problems of question form that are of internal interest to the practice of social research and to criminological research in particular. If questions are well formed, we are well on the way toward finding an answer, if, that is, one can be found. Certainly, until the question is "properly" stated, "proper" research strategies cannot be developed. It is, I am sure, not my experience alone, but it seems to be a characteristic of any research with which I have been associated and that could be said to have any measure of success, that the questions as first stated were revised at least once as the project progressed. In more than one case, the initial statement of the problem was so inappropriate for research analysis (though it seemed plausible enough) that any results deriving from following the course indicated by such question form would have resulted in only misleading answers. Finding the appropriate question form is not an easy matter for the experienced social research scientist. It cannot be surprising, therefore, that the general public gets its questions wrong.

It may be accepted that there is difficulty with the statement of research-type questions that nonetheless relate to the public opinion style questions and are of concern to the public administrator and politician. Clearly, some rules are required whereby the qualities of appropriately formed question statements may be recognized. We may agree with Dr. Pell, but ask what he may have meant by "well-stated" questions. His invocation of "logic" and "mother-wit" are no more than the typically unhelpful exhortations of his period.

I shall attempt to set forth some tests of "appropriateness" relating to the form of research questions in the public policy sector. It is, of course, not possible to modify the structure of questions unless there are some rules whereby the terms, phrases, or constructs can be assessed. A question that has not been formed into a recognized linguistic structure cannot be tested. It follows, therefore, that prior to the stage at which thinking has to be communicated to others and the questions take form in common language, each individual research scientist is expected to use his or her personal imagination in a way that he or she recognizes as his or her own most effective approach—by visual or verbal analogue or any other means. Each research question formed for each proposed research inquiry is like the classical hypothesis. It must be stated before it can be subject to test, and if it fails to meet the tests, it can be rejected. If it is rejected, it is "back to the imagination" to frame another question that may withstand the testing.

It is suggested that the major problem of the form of questions in social research is that the public (and some research workers) state the research questions in the language of answers. That is to say, the same kind of language that is used to describe the results of the research is used to state the questions. This may sound negative, vague, or possibly incorrect. Negative it must be, because that is how the scientific method approached propositions. The vagueness, it is hoped, will be dispelled as we discuss some examples.

ANSWER-LANGUAGE QUESTIONS

The rule proposed is quite simply stated—answer-language is not appropriate for the statement of research questions. The test, then, is to seek to identify any answer-language in the phrasing. If it is identified, then a reformulation of the question is called for. If it is possible to state questions only in this form, then there is something more seriously wrong in the thinking in the particular field concerned. (If we may anticipate the concluding features of this chapter, this comment will lead us to rethink the concept of "crime" in order to deal with "crime.")

The inappropriate "language of answers" is somewhat similar to "begging the question," but is more sophisticated and less easy to recognize. One or two examples may suffice to demonstrate this. More serious difficulties may be expected when the questions relate to topics with emotional and political overtones. Because of its proximity to the economic sector, there are simple, reasoned examples in the field of occupational psychology. An example from this field may, perhaps, be apposite and adequate.

A manufacture might, say, approach an industrial consultant and state that he or she "has a staff training problem" and request that the consultant work out a "training package" for his or her needs. This approach may well be stimulated because our manufacturer is aware that a competitor had such a "package" prepared by consultants. Any consultant firm that went along with a kit of training materials might find some acceptance with the customer, at least initially, but would receive little approval from the discipline of industrial psychology. The statement of the problem (a "staff training problem") represents the statement of the problem in terms of the language of answers. Perhaps this is too simple and obvious. Nonetheless, the manufacturer, it may be thought, should know his or her business and be able to request the kind of research needed. Why then is this form of specification of research problems unacceptable? This may become clear by reference to another example. A different firm in the same kind of business might seek advice, stating that they had "a staff selection problem." Some consultants might accept this commission and go along with a package of "selection materials" such as aptitude tests and interview training manuals.

These approaches are similar and both are equally inappropriate. The specification of the problem in terms of the answers is a specification for failure. It will be obvious that the "selection" problem (as specified by the customer in the language of answers) might turn out to be a "training" problem and the training problem might be a "selection" problem. Or, in each case, there may be problems of each kind or of neither kind. Specification of the problems in terms of the language of answers seems to be a rather popular form of attempted communication between administrators and scientists. It seems to appeal both to "customers" and to research workers seeking funds from many foundations and agencies.

A somewhat less obvious example will illustrate a serious underlying misunderstanding that gives rise most frequently to the specification of problems in answer-language. This is the widespread belief, among decision makers in almost every field, that if only they had sufficient sound information they could make better decisions. The problems of decision making are thus specified in terms of supposed answers, the relevant information being more quickly accessible. The problems of decision makers may have little or nothing to do with the quantity or even the quality of the available information, and certainly are most improbably related to the speed with which information can be accessed. (It may be that computer salespeople have encouraged this misconception!) Because dichotomous views of the world predominate, the difficulty, it is thought, must be in one or other—the individual or the data provided. But as will be seen later, there are other possible explanations of decision deficiencies.

There are many reasons for the apparent popularity of the phrasing of research questions in answer-type language. The layperson may be more likely to think that he or she understands the project when its workings are expressed in this form, while to those who see themselves as "customers" it suggests a more tangible product as the likely outcome. The research worker may resort to this form of language when accused of obfuscating issues by jargon. There is no doubt of the attractiveness of the language of answers, and its main danger is in its subtle appeal.

DANGEROUSLY SIMPLE AND ATTRACTIVELY DANGEROUS

Perhaps it may be accepted that there are rules for distinguishing "good" research questions from "poor" research questions, but it may not be obvious how "good" questions would be more likely than others to provide answers that would find a ready acceptance with policy-makers. It is at this point that the difficulties of communication between scientists and administrators become the more apparent and significant. Much social research that originates in the research community begins with a not-too-well-formed idea closely linked with a search for money. There is strong belief among social scientists that unless they can give assurances of a specific outcome, and express this as a "pay-off," no funds will be obtained. Unfortunately this belief has proved to be reasonably correct, and may well be at the root of many problems social scientists have in establishing the credibility of their disciplines.

Research that is designed to have obvious pay-offs cannot be daring. Predictable outcomes will be trivial outcomes. If more than trivial outcomes are promised, the probability that they will be realized will be small. But, that has been the story of much recent criminal justice research; promises were made of outcomes that were thought to be pleasing to those in charge of funds. These promises were not kept. Those who made the most striking promises were the most likely to obtain the funds, but by the same token, were the least likely to deliver important or useful findings. But there is a more deep-seated reason for the promises of desirable outcomes. Often promises made by social scientists are based upon beliefs that they regard as rational and their arguments convince themselves as well as those providing the money. Social research workers often subscribe to the belief that those things that are socially desirable—"good things"—must be compatible with "sound" knowledge. The idea is widespread that "beauty is truth, truth beauty" (if only we could find enough evidence). One example of this background of belief, which has had serious negative consequences for criminological research and humanitarian policy, is the belief that "enlightened treatment" of offenders must result in lower recidivism rates. Research began to be linked with claims that humanitarian methods (group therapy, work release, family visits, and such) must be effective in reformation of those incarcerated. Hence the public interest would be served by adopting these approaches, and research would "prove" how effective they were. What was seen as "right" (i.e., humanitarian) was also assumed to be scientifically true; a view similar to that underpinning psychoanalysis that self-realization cures. Nettler (1961) has pointed out that there is neither philosophical support nor empirical evidence for this perspective. There is no necessary association between that which is ethically correct and that which is scientifically sound.

There are other difficulties in social research that are associated with ideological perspectives. For example, the *New Criminology* is regarded by some as a methodological argument, while about equal numbers see it as an ideological conflict of values. No one lives without value preferences and all make value choices. Neither social policy nor social research can be "value free." Research workers must be careful to recognize the assumptions they may import into projects; they should select methods that will, as far as possible, insulate them from prejudicial judgments. The bias of value choice may be reduced by good methodology, but it cannot be eliminated and should, therefore, be noted. The problems of potential bias do not rest solely at the interface between the customer and the client—between the policymakers and research workers. Directors of research establishments also may transform issues into the language of their familiar discipline at the expense of precision. Sociologists may prefer specifications that emphasize sociological concepts while psychologists may stress individual personality factors, and so on. On occasions, that which is easy to measure is measured, even though it may be poor proxy for that which should be assessed. Before we seek to sort out these problems of social research policy it is necessary to consider a few more related difficulties.

PURPOSE STATEMENTS

The specification of a question in the language of answers is similar to the specification of operations in terms of "closed systems" models. That is to say, the problem is seen as arising within certain organizational bounds and the solutions are expected to be contained within the same boundaries. Sound research cannot recognize boundaries of allocated power (responsibility?) and this represents another difficulty in the customer/client roles of administrator and scientist. It must be acknowledged that the problems of the world are not divided up in the same ways as are government departments or university disciplines. But this does not need to be elaborated here.

While it is true that the objective sought in a research project does not constrain the form of language of the research questions—quite inappropriate questions may be well expressed—there is an interaction between the question form and the objective, which will be illustrated by two examples.

Donald Schon has pointed out that when a certain form of sandal manufacturers sought marketing research assistance they received advice that they should not regard themselves as in the business of the manufacture and sale of sandals, but as in the leisure footwear business. The central theme of the business (that which set the tone of all proceedings at board meetings) was to be changed from a focus on sandals to a focus on leisure footwear. Does this seem a trivial play upon words or a significant reorientation of policy? Is the advice parallel to calling garbage collectors "environmental officers?" Consider another example of exactly the same kind of linguistic transformation as that which transformed sandals into leisure footwear. Imagine a company that manufactured soap, marketed soap, and saw itself as in the "soap manufacturing business." Suppose that this all took place before the development of detergents. Now assume that this soap manufacturing company requested the assistance of the same marketing consultants and received exactly similar advice, namely, they should not see themselves as in the business of the manufacture and sale of soap, but as in the business of manufacturing and selling cleansing agents. Now, along come detergents! This firm now sees detergents (as indeed they are) as cleansing agents. They are in the business of cleansing agents, therefore, detergents are their concern—it is their business. To them the policy is clear; detergents are to be considered positively and possibly manufactured and marketed. But a rival firm in the soap business, which continued to regard itself as "in the soap industry," would be expected to regard detergents as the enemy, certainly not to be welcomed because they were "in soap." As we know from history, such a firm would soon have been in the financial "soup." In the latter case, the problem, namely, selling soap was specified in terms of the kind of answers: They must also relate to soap. Detergents are not soap, therefore, they are in the wrong kind of answer set. The specification of purpose by function can break this constraint of thought. Indeed, much the same idea might have been intended by the theme, popularized some years ago with the slogan, "management by objectives." However, objectives can still be spelled out in the language of sandals and soap! We are concerned with the end purpose to be served, which in government means the public interest, and we would hope that public interest means peoples' interest.

CONTRACTS, CUSTOMERS, AND PUBLIC OPINION

The idea of "product image" and similar constructs of marketing have become familiar concepts. The concept of "image" not only applies to individual products and styles of packaging, but it extends to outlets. In England no problem of image, it seems, arose from the introduction of the sale of foods (in close proximity to clothing and other consumer goods) in stores whose reputation had been built on sound clothing products. When similar marketing was attempted in Canada (where food stores could sell certain kitchen items and some hardware without difficulty) the introduction of food into "clothing" stores did not appeal to the customers.

One of the first tasks of the social research worker who wishes to work in the field of criminology may be to ascertain the nature of the "image" the role presents, and to find a means to correct or modify that image. Many problems arise from poor communication. Poor communication has a tendency to begin and amplify out of incorrect assumptions that may not be recognized by either party. Social research sounds to many to be close to "socialism," and the term *socialism* evokes emotional reaction; generally negative. The criminologist, as we noted earlier, "does" criminology, and in so doing does little that the public thinks needs to be done. This fact has less impact than it might because the public has few correct opinions as to what criminology is, and hence an incorrect "image" of the "criminologist." In England and some other countries, for example, the description "criminologist" is applied by the mass media to a detective or crime-solving specialist (concerned solely with "Who did it?"), as well as to pathologists and social scientists from disciplines of psychology, sociology, jurisprudence, and others who carry out a wide range of research concerning crime and criminals. A social scientist announcing himself to a lay audience as a "criminologist" would be expected to tell stories of manhunts, almost perfect crimes, swindles in high places, and the kind of material that fills the paperback crime novel. If the announcement were in other terms (those that would be adequate descriptions in academic circles), there would still be a wide gap between the experience, skill, and techniques expected or attributed, and those that the individual would claim.

The use of the term *image* in relation to the identification of roles of research worker and administrator is intended to imply that the problem of communication is not one that can be corrected merely by the use of the correct language. As McLuhan pointed out, the medium—which can be the individual encoding the message—is (part of) that message. Or, as was said earlier, "what you are" (meaning, of course, what I perceive you to be) "speaks so loudly that I cannot hear what you say." Communication takes place, as it were, between the research worker and both visible and invisible audiences. The audiences for the social scientist include his colleagues and mentors (possibly "invisible"), as well as his "customers." By *invisible audience* we mean the various levels of accountability that the scientist acknowledges for the quality of his work and the ethics of his procedures.

The total audience for the products of research in the social policy area is wider and involves very different interests from those that characterize most other scientific research activities. Physicists, astronomers, chemists, mathematicians, and physicians have fewer problems with diversity of "audiences" and presumptions of accountability. In the course of their research they are less likely to offend politicians, and the press is likely to treat them with reserve, if not respect. Any conflicts that arise within these and similar disciplines, while powerful and even vicious, will tend to be restricted to the participants and a small audience. Not so for the social scientist, and certainly not for the criminologist. Should a controversy develop in this field of interest, almost everybody will try to get into the fight. No experience is regarded as necessary and any serious knowledge of the subject may serve only as an embarrassment! The less informed in the subject matter are the participants, the more certain they will be that they are right. The "general public" (in some form or another) will often be on the sidelines whenever any social research effort reaches any major proportions. At times, the "customer" for the research (such as a government department) will be extremely sensitive to their particular readings of the invisible audience—the general "public opinion." This invisible audience may become too visible should anything seem to go wrong with the research or its implementation.

ACCOUNTABILITY

Social scientists who work in the public sector may be regarded as ultimately responsible to the public in accordance with the prevailing theory of democratic government. Moreover, since they are concerned with investigations that they might reasonably expect to have an impact upon public policy, they will share many concerns with the policymakers. The range of their accountability is wider than that which applies to social scientists in industry and commerce. Clearly, both industry and commerce make extensive use of social research, and if there were no intention of making use of the results, there would be no market for such research. Research may not get started for a variety of reasons, but there is little likelihood in the private sector that the results will be ignored.

The interface between the likely uses of the results of research and the formulation of the research questions in the first instance is significant though not simple. The purpose for which research is commissioned, in turn, is linked with the concept of public interest, and through this construct to the idea of accountability. The idea of accountability of public servants, whether scientists or administrators, is a complex issue. But as we move from one level of concept to another, the impact upon our immediate concern, namely, the design of research questions—becomes more and more attenuated.

In public policy matters, research is often carried out in universities by those who see their public as more extensive than the immediate "customer." Those who carry out their research in other locations may feel that some of the accountability function devolves less upon them than upon others in their organization. We shall not argue this point, but it is interesting to note, before returning to the technology of question form, that for those engaged in social research, many levels of accountability may be distinguished. Seven categories may be proposed, namely: (1) the subjects involved, (2) the research worker's colleagues in the same organization, (3) the management or the customer for research, (4) the legislative body, (5) the professional(s) concerned, (6) the general public, and (7) the research worker himself or herself. Some of these categories might need to be subdivided to provide a more satisfactory account of the levels involved in certain organizations. Only in one or two countries has only one of these categories been formally considered by the appointed democratic institutions. In the United States and some other countries, legislation exists to protect the rights of persons who may become the subjects of research, and though not frequently relevant to social research, there are rules regarding the protection of animals. (Some have suggested that the latter have received more attention than certain categories of persons.)

It is not possible here to explore equally the consequences for research design of each of the posited levels of accountability. The "customer" (whether government body or other) and the "general public" are the categories of most significance in relation to the implementation of criminological research. While we shall concentrate upon these levels of accountability, we recognize that, from different perspectives, each level of accountability is of very considerable importance to the practice of social research.

Concepts of accountability influence the form and style of research questions because research workers are responsive in their beliefs about their "public." They may harbor some doubts as to the possibility of delivering a "product" in the way considered to be necessary to frame their promises in the drafting of the research proposal. When faced with a challenge from a colleague to this effect, the proposal writer may often seek to justify his or her action by saying that once the research is funded, the precise details will be "negotiable." Whether it is possible to "negotiate" from a poorly specified research to a sound product may depend upon many things, not the least of which is the self-image of the customer. It may be that the scientist has incorrectly assessed his or her customer's viewpoint. If so, remedies lie in improved communications between research producers and consumers. On the other hand, it is possible that it is the customer who has an inappropriate image not only of research, but also of the kinds of operations in which his or her own organization is involved. In the latter case, the methods of specification of question form are irrelevant—right or wrong, research cannot be successful if it is directed toward an inappropriate target.

CONSEQUENCES OF LINGUISTIC PRECISION

Perhaps it may be claimed that we have shown, in a general way, that getting the words right is of great importance for business, policymaking, and research. So far the discussion has used examples from commerce and industrial management. It is time to turn again to crime and to consider the consequences of applying the general principles suggested by our examples from other fields. The general purpose of criminology is to "understand" crime. But the subjective satisfaction of scientists—their belief that they understand a phenomenon—is not a criterion of sound scientific work. It may be that the general public has a point when it claims that those who deal with crime should seek to reduce its incidence and serious consequences. If research workers make a claim that they have improved their understanding of any phenomenon, it seems reasonable to assume that more or better ways are now known whereby it can be predicted and controlled. We cannot observe anyone's "understanding," and we need some means whereby we can be convinced of scientific claims. Claims that relate to knowledge of *crime* presuppose that we know what we mean by the use of that word. But though pressures are brought to bear upon politicians to "do something" about "crime," different sectors of the public mean different things by this demand. To some, abortion at the option of the mother-to-be is not only a sin, but a serious crime; and, indeed, in some countries, it is. To others, homosexual activities are or should be crimes. Some argue that drug abuse is a medical matter, others that it is criminal. What, then, is "crime"?

Recalling Hyman Gross's view to which we made reference early in this chapter, can we agree that no one needs to refer to law books to know that "murder is a crime"? Of course, we must acknowledge that "murder" is a crime. Killing is not a crime—only certain kinds of killings. Indeed, in order to know what acts of killing may be called "murder" we have only one source, namely, the law of the country concerned. It is only in that specific law that the word *murder* is defined. There is no international meaning to the term *murder*, even in countries that use the English language. Thus Gross's comment is tautological because if we can say that an act was in fact "murder" we must have memorized the definition from "the (appropriate) law books"—there is no other way of knowing. But even within the law of one single state the definition can be uncertain. The courts may determine that a particular act, which in the preceding stages of criminal process was classified as "murder," was, in fact, some lesser crime. Presumably, the classification of an act as "murder" by the trial has a higher standing than any other prior definition, and the court of appeal a still higher standing? So we must assume that the last decision as to the classification of an act as a crime, or as a particular category of crime, is the definition that is "correct." This raises difficulties because most cases drop out of the decision network before a high-level assessment of the facts has been made. Furthermore, as the case proceeds through the system, it is likely that more information will become available. Classification is, then, some function of the amount of information available and the level of decision process reached, and these will be operationally correlated. Much of the room of maneuver that prosecutors have in negotiating a plea is in the act of defining—of calling a particular action a particular name. The naming (category allocation) will determine the limits of punishment that can be inflicted upon the individual concerned.

The close connection between criminal law and social control is through penal sanctions. While other divisions of government authority can seek to exact penalties for noncompliance with regulation, it is the final sanction of criminal law that, as it were, stands behind the other penalty systems. Some harmful acts, particularly those of corporate bodies, have switched from criminal law to administrative and civil law over the years. The arguments in the legislative assemblies in relation to these changes are most informative. If we ignore military or martial law, the criminal justice system has unique power of punishment. Despite this, and the fact that the law declares (i.e., defines) certain described acts as "crimes," it is not the law that "makes" an act a crime. Rather, crimes are "made" by the use of the concept that the particular acts justify invoking those penal sanctions that are the preserve of the criminal justice system. An action is not morally wrong because it is against the law. It is not the law that "drives" the idea of justification of punishment, but the idea of justified punishment that "drives" the criminal law. Certain acts are seen as justifying punishment, and in order that an appropriate (morally justified) punishment may be inflicted, the act must be brought within the authority of that system of government that is empowered to apply that punishment. So, when people say that a particular act "ought to be a crime" they mean that, in their view, it is an act that deserves a punishment that can be administered only through the criminal system. Thus calling an act a "crime" tells us little or nothing about the act itself, but it tells us precisely what (if it is possible) will be done about it. It will be processed through the criminal justice system.

Have we not seen that kind of statement of problems before?

Does not the very use of the term *crime* take us immediately into the language of soap and sandals—the "language of answers," which we have seen provides a completely unsatisfactory basis for analysis? Perhaps this is a fundamental problem with the study of "crime"? For many kinds of analysis, I would take the view that this is so. If, however, we cease to be true believers in the construct of "crime" (e.g., the *mala in se* doctrine); if, rather we see as our focus of analysis the processes of selecting, describing, and defining certain acts as "crimes," we will be moving in a decision research framework. This form of framework will prove more satisfactory than one that attached to events the meaning of "criminal" and ignores by whom, and the mechanism whereby, these acts were so classified.

CONSUMERISM IN CRIMINOLOGY

The early editions of Pearson's Tables for Statisticians and Biometricians included as a frontispiece a quotation attributed to Lord Kelvin:

> When you can measure what you are speaking about and express it in numbers, you know something about it, but when you cannot measure it, when you cannot express it in numbers, your knowledge is of a meagre and unsatisfactory kind.

The key phrase is clearly, "what you are speaking about." What precisely are we speaking about when we speak of "crime"? If we isolate some of these, then we may know what we are speaking about and hence "know something about it." We have seen that the initial trigger is the division to process the act and if possible, the actor, through the machinery of the "criminal justice system." Once entered, this "machine" (which is appropriately pictured as a decision network) controls various transitions. Each transition is a decision to "take the case further." Thus an arrest/summons is a response to the stimulus of a complaint, a prosecution is a response to the stimulus of an arrest, a finding of guilty/not guilty is a response to a prosecution, and so on. No stimuli are well measured by mere responses to them. Indeed, it is not possible to identify changes in the impact of varying responses if our only measurement is the response. Apart from sample survey data, the crime system defines and controls its own input. Effective monitoring of a system requires some information input from sources external to that system.

There is a strong case for the application of "Nadarism" (i.e., aggressive consumer advocacy) to the criminal justice system from the initial input to the output. This is intended to cover all of the varieties of "consumers" of the system—the prison officer as well as the incarcerated offender; the police as well as the "public." In particular, this proposal is not intended to mean merely that crude readings of public opinion should determine what is done, nor does it mean that public opinion should be ignored.

When the public demands that "something be done about crime" they are making a claim upon the social mechanisms of the country; not only upon the criminal justice system, because, as we have noted, the public do not know what crime is. The public wants protection from harms—the public wants as high a level of quality of life as possible. Quality of life for the public relates to quality of service of government agencies.

REFERENCES

Abercrombie, N., S. Hill, and B. S. Turner
1984 *The Penguin Dictionary of Sociology*. Middlesex, England: Penguin.

Adler, F.
1975 *Sisters in Crime: The Rise of the New Female Criminal*. New York: McGraw-Hill.

Aichhorn, A.
1936 *Wayward Youth*. New York: Viking.

Akers, R.
1964 "Socio-economic status and delinquent behavior: A retest." *Journal of Research in Crime and Delinquency* 1: 38-46.

Allport, G. W.
1962 "The general and the unique in psychological science." *Journal of Personality* 30: 405-522.

Almond, B. and S. Verba
1963 *Civil Culture*. Princeton, NJ: Princeton University Press.

Aron, R.
1968 *Main Currents in Sociological Thought* (Vol. 1). Garden City, NY: Doubleday.

Bachman, J. G., R. L. Kahn, M. T. Mednick, T. N. Davidson, and L. D.Johnston
1967 *Youth in Transition* (Vol. 1). Ann Arbor: University of Michigan, Institute for Social Research.

Bachman, J. G., P. O'Malley, and L. Johnston
1978 *Adolescence to Adulthood: Change and Stability in the Lives of Young Men*. Ann Arbor: University of Michigan, Institute for Social Research.

Baldwin, J.
1979 "Ecological and areal studies in Great Britain and the United States," in N. Morris and M. Tonry (eds.) *Crime and Justice* (Vol. 1). Chicago: University of Chicago Press.

Balkwell, J.
1983 *Metropolitan Structure and Violent Crime: A Further Examination of the Blau and Blau Relative Deprivation Thesis*. Presented at the annual meeting of American Society of Criminology, Denver, CO.

Ball-Rokeach, S.
1973 "Values and violence: A test of the subculture of violence thesis." *American Sociological Review* 38: 736-749.

Bandura, A.
1977 *Social Learning Theory*. Englewood Cliffs, NJ: Prentice-Hall.

Beccaria, C.
1963 *On Crimes and Punishments*. New York: Bobbs-Merrill.

Becker, G.
1968 "Crime and punishment: An economic approach." *Journal of Political Economy* 76: 169.

Becker, H.
1963 "Deviance as a master status," in H. Becker (ed.) *Outsiders*. New York: Free Press.

Bentham, J.
1843 "Principles of penal law," Part II, Book 1, Chap. 3 in J. Bowring (ed.) *The Works of Jeremy Bentham*. New York: Russell & Russell.

Berk, R. A., K. J. Lenihan, and P. H. Rossi
1980 "Crime and poverty: Some experimental evidence from ex-offenders." *American Sociological Review* 45: 766-786.

Berry, B. and J. Kasarda
1977 *Contemporary Urban Ecology*. New York: Macmillan.

Blalock, H.
1967 *A Theory of Minority Relations*. New York: John Wiley.
1970 *An Introduction to Social Research*. Englewood Cliffs, NJ: Prentice-Hall.

Blau, J. and P. Blau
1982 "The cost of inequality: Metropolitan structure and violent crime." *American Sociological Review* 47: 114-129.

Blau, P.
1977 *Inequality and Heterogeneity*. New York: Free Press.
1981 "Behavioral science or behavioral sociology?" *American Sociologist* 16: 170-171.

Blumenthal, M., R. L. Kahn, F. Andrews, M. Frank, and R. B. Head
1972 *Justifying Violence*. Ann Arbor: University of Michigan, Institute for Social Research.

Blumstein, A. and E. Graddy
1982 "Prevalence and recidivism in index arrests: A feedback model." *Law and Society Review* 16: 265-290.

Bonger, W.
1969 *Criminality and Economic Conditions*. Bloomington: Indiana University Press.

Bookin-Weiner, H. and R. Horowitz
1983 "The end of the youth gang: Fad or facts?" *Criminology* 21: 585-602.

Bovet, L.
1951 *Psychiatric Aspects of Juvenile Delinquency*. Geneva: World Health Organization.

Braithwaite, J.
1979 *Inequality, Crime and Public Policy*. London: Routledge & Kegan Paul.
1981 "The myth of social class and criminality reconsidered." *American Sociological Review* 46: 36-57.

Braithwaite, J. and D. Biles
1980 "Crime victimization in Australia: A comparison with the U.S." *Journal of Crime and Justice* 3: 95-110.

Brenner, H.
1976a *Estimating the Social Costs of National Economic Policy: Implications for Mental and Physical Health and Criminal Aggression*. Washington, DC: Government Printing Office.
1976b *Effects of the National Economy on Criminal Aggression: II*. Final Report. Rockville, MD: National Institute of Mental Health.

Buffalo, M. D. and J. Rodgers
1971 "Behavioral norms, moral norms and attachment: Problems of deviance and conformity." *Social Problems* 19: 101-113.

Bursik, R.
1983 *Sources of Change in the Delinquency Rates of Chicago's Local Communities 1940-1980.* Presented at the annual meeting of the American Society of Criminology, Denver, CO.

Byrne, J.
1983 *Ecological Correlates of Property Crime in the United States: An Intercity Analysis.* Presented at the annual meeting of the American Society of Criminology, Denver, CO.
1984 "The ecological/nonecological debate reconsidered," in J. Byrne and R. Sampson (eds.) *The Social Ecology of Crime: Theory, Research, and Public Policy.* New York: Verlag-Springer.

Cantril, H.
1965 *The Patterns of Human Concerns.* New Brunswick, NJ: Rutgers University Press.

Carroll, L. and P. Jackson
1983 "Inequality, opportunity, and crime rates in central cities." *Criminology* 21: 178-194.

Carter, R. L. and K. Q. Hill
1979 *The Criminal's Image of the City.* New York: Pergamon.

Cernkovich, S. and P. Giordano
1979 "A comparative analysis of male and female delinquency." *Sociological Quarterly* 20: 131-145.

Chambliss, W. and R. Seidman
1971 *Law, Order, and Power.* Reading, MA: Addison-Wesley.

Clark, J. and E. Wenninger
1962 "Socioeconomic class and area as correlates of illegal behavior among juveniles." *American Sociological Review* 28: 826-834.

Clarke, R. V.
1983 "Situational crime prevention: Its theoretical basis and practical scope," in N. Morris and M. Tonry (eds.) *Crime and Justice* (Vol. 4). Chicago: University of Chicago Press.

Clarke, R. V. and D. Cornish
1985 "Modeling offenders' decisions: A framework for research and policy," in N. Morris and M. Tonry (eds.) *Crime and Justice* (Vol. 6). Chicago: University of Chicago Press.

Cloward, R. A. and L. Ohlin
1960 *Delinquency and Opportunity.* New York: Free Press.

Cohen, A. K.
1955 *Delinquent Boys.* New York: Free Press.

Cohen, L. E. and D. Cantor
1980 "The determinants of larceny: An empirical and theoretical study." *Journal of Research in Crime and Delinquency* 17 (2): 140-159.
1981 "Residential burglary in the United States: Life-style and demographic factors associated with the probability of victimization." *Journal of Research in Crime and Delinquency* 18 (1): 113-127.

Cohen, L. E., D. Cantor, and J. R. Kluegel
1981 "Robbery victimization in the United States: An analysis of a nonrandom event." *Social Science Quarterly* 62: 644-657.
Cohen, L. E. and M. Felson
1979a "Social change and crime rate trends: A routine activities approach." *American Sociological Review* 44: 558-607.
1979b "Estimating the social costs of national economic policy: A critical examination of the Brenner study." *Social Indicators Research* 6 (2): 251-259.
Cohen, L. E., M. Felson, and K. C. Land
1980 "Property crime rates in the United States: A macrodynamic analysis 1947-1977; with ex ante forecasts for the mid-1980's." *American Journal of Sociology* 86 (1): 98-118.
Cohen, L., J. Kluegel, and K. Land
1981 "Social inequality and predatory criminal victimization: An exposition and test of a formal theory." *American Sociological Review* 46: 505-524.
Coleman, J. S.
1968 "The mathematical study of change," in H. Blalock and A. Blalock (eds.) *Methodology in Social Research.* New York: McGraw-Hill.
Conklin, J. E.
1971 "Criminal environment and support for the law." *Law and Society Review* 6: 247-259.
Cornish, D. and R. V. Clarke
1986 *The Reasoning Criminal.* New York: Verlag-Springer.
Corrado, R. R., R. Roesch, W. Glackman, J. L. Evans, and G. J. Ledger
1980 "Life styles and personal victimization: A test of the model with Canadian survey data." *Journal of Crime and Justice* 3: 129-139.
Crutchfield, R., M. Geerken, and W. Gove
1982 "Crime rates and social integration: The impact of metropolitan mobility." *Criminology* 20: 467-478.
DeFronzo, J.
1983 "Economic assistance to impoverished Americans: Relationship to incidence of crime." *Criminology* 21: 119-136.
Dentler, R. A. and L. J. Monroe
1961 "Social correlates of early adolescent theft." *American Sociological Review* 26: 733-743.
Dewey, J. and A. F. Bentley
1949 *Knowing and the Known.* Boston: Beacon.
Duffee, D.
1980 *Explaining Criminal Justice: Community Theory and Criminal Justice Reform.* Cambridge, MA: Oelgeschalager, Gunn & Hain.
Dunn, C.
1980 "Crime area research," in D. George-Abeyie and K. Harries (eds.) *Crime: A Spatial Perspective.* New York: Columbia University Press.
Durkheim, E.
1951 *Suicide.* New York: Free Press.
Elliott, D. S. and S. Ageton
1980 "Reconciling race and class differences in self-reported and official estimates of delinquency." *American Sociological Review* 1: 95-110.

Elliott, D. S. and D. Huizinga
1983 "Social class and delinquent behavior in a national youth study." *Criminology* 21: 109-117.
Elliott, D. S., B. A. Knowles, and R. J. Canter
1981 *The Epidemiology of Delinquent Behavior and Drug Use Among American Adolescents, 1976-1978*. A report of the National Youth Survey (Project Report No. 14). Boulder, CO: Behavioral Research Institute.
Elliott, D. S. and H. L. Voss
1974 *Delinquency and Dropout*. Lexington, MA: Lexington Books.
Empey, L. T.
1978 *American Delinquency*. Homewood, IL: Dorsey.
Empey, L. T. and S. G. Lubeck
1971 *Explaining Delinquency*. Lexington, MA: Lexington Books.
Erickson, M. L. and L. T. Empey
1965 "Class position, peers and delinquency." *Sociology and Social Research* 49 (April): 268-282.
Eysenck, H.
1977 *Crime and Personality*. London: Routledge & Kegan Paul.
Faris, R.E.L.
1979 *Chicago Sociology 1920-1932* (reprint of 1967 ed.). Chicago: University of Chicago Press.
Farrington, D.
1979 "Environmental stress, delinquent behavior, and convictions," in I. G. Sarason and C. D. Spielberger (eds.) *Stress and Anxiety* (Vol. 6). Washington, DC: Hemisphere.
Feagin, J.
1973 "Community disorganization: Some critical notes." *Sociological Inquiry* 43: 123-145.
Fellin, P. and E. Litwak
1963 "Neighborhood cohesion under conditions of mobility." *American Sociological Review* 28: 364-376.
Felson, M., L. E. Cohen, and K. C. Land
1978 *Forecasting Models for Index Crime Rates*. Unpublished grant application, National Institute of Mental Health.
Ferri, E.
1917 *Criminal Sociology. Boston: Little, Brown.*
1968 "Three lectures," in S. Grupp (ed.) The Positive School of Criminology. Pittsburgh: University of Pittsburgh Press.
1973 "Polemica in difesa della scvola criminale postitiva" as cited in T. Sellin "Enrico Ferri" in H. Mannheim (ed.) *Pioneers in Criminology*. Montclair, NJ: Patterson Smith.
Fischer, C.
1975 "Toward a subcultural theory of urbanism." *American Journal of Sociology* 80 (6): 1319-1341.
1981 "The public and private worlds of city life." *American Sociological Review* 46: 306-316.
Frederics, M. A. and M. Molnar
1969 "Relative occupational anticipations and aspirations of delinquents and nondelinquents." *Journal of Research in Crime and Delinquency* 6: 1-7.

Freud, S.

1961 *Civilization and Its Discontents.* New York: W. W. Norton.

Gans, H. J.

1962 "Urbanism and suburbanism as ways of life: A reevaluation of definitions," in A. M. Rose (ed.) *Human Behavior and Social Processes.* Boston, MA: Houghton Mifflin.

Garofalo, J.

1981 "The fear of crime: Causes and consequences." *Journal of Criminal Law and Criminology* 72 (2): 829-857.

Garofalo, J. and M. J. Hindelang

1977 *An Introduction to the National Crime Survey.* Washington, DC: Government Printing Office.

Glueck, S. and E. Glueck

1950 *Unraveling Juvenile Delinquency.* Cambridge, MA: Harvard University Press.

Gold, M.

1970 *Delinquent Behavior in an American City.* Belmont, CA: Brooks/Cole.

Gordon, R. A.

1967 "Issues in the ecological study of delinquency." *American Sociological Review* 32: 927-944.

1979 "Prevalence: The rare datum in delinquency measurement and its implications for the theory of delinquency," in M. W. Klein (ed.) *The Juvenile Justice System.* Newbury Park, CA: Sage.

Gordon, R., J. F. Short, D. Cartwright, and F. Strodtbeck

1963 "Values and gang delinquency." *American Journal of Sociology* 69: 109-128.

Gottfredson, M. R.

1981 "On the etiology of criminal victimization." *Journal of Criminal Law and Criminology* 72 (2): 712-726.

1982 "The social scientist and rehabilitative crime policy." *Criminology* 20 (May): 29-42.

Gould, L. C.

1969 "Who defines delinquency? A comparison of self-reported and officially reported indices of delinquency for three racial groups." *Social Problems* 16: 325-336.

Gould, S. J.

1981 *The Mismeasure of Man.* New York: W. W. Norton.

Granovetter, M.

1973 "The strength of weak ties." *American Journal of Sociology* 78: 1360-1380.

Greenberg, D. (ed.)

1981 *Crime and Capitalism.* Palo Alto, CA: Mayfield.

Greenberg, S., W. Rohe, and J. Williams

1982 *The Relationship Between Informal Social Control, Neighborhood Crime, and Fear: A Synthesis and Assessment of the Research.* Presented at the annual meeting of the American Society of Criminology, Toronto, Canada.

Gross, H.

1979 *A Theory of Justice.* New York: Oxford University Press.

Hannan, M. T.

1971 *Aggregation and Disaggregation in Sociology.* Lexington, MA: Lexington Books.

Hathaway, S. R. and E. D. Monachesi
1963 *Adolescent Personality and Behavior: MMPI Patterns of Normal, Delinquent Dropout, and Other Outcomes.* Minneapolis: University of Minnesota Press.
Hauser, R.
1970 "Context and consex: A cautionary tale." *American Journal of Sociology* 75: 645-664.
Havighurst, R. J.
1962 *Growing Up in River City.* New York: John Wiley.
Healy, W.
1915 *The Individual Delinquent.* Boston: Little, Brown.
Healy, W. and A. F. Bronner
1969 *New Light on Delinquency and Its Treatment.* New Haven, CT: Yale University Press.
Hepburn, J. R.
1976 "Casting alternative models of delinquency causation." *Journal of Criminal Law and Criminology* 67 (December): 450-460.
Hindelang, M. J.
1973 "Causes of delinquency: A partial replication and extension." *Social Problems* 20: 471-487.
1974 "The uniform crime reports revisited." *Journal of Criminal Justice* 2: 1-18.
1976 *Criminal Victimization in Eight American Cities: A Descriptive Analysis of Common Theft and Assault.* Cambridge, MA: Ballinger.
1978 "Race and involvement in common law personal crimes." *American Sociological Review* 43: 93-109.
1980 "Sex differences in criminal activity." *Social Problems* 27: 143-156.
1981 "Variations in sex-race-age-specific incidence rates of offending." *American Sociological Review* 46: 461-474.
Hindelang, M. J., M. R. Gottfredson, and J. Garofalo
1978 *Victims of Personal Crime: An Empirical Foundation for a Theory of Personal Victimization.* Cambridge, MA: Ballinger.
Hindelang, M., T. Hirschi, and J. Weis
1981 *Measuring Delinquency.* Newbury Park, CA: Sage.
1979 "Correlates of delinquency: The illusion of discrepancy between self-report and official measures." *American Sociological Review* 44: 995-1014.
Hindelang, M. J. and M. J. McDermott
1981 *Juvenile Criminal Behavior: An Analysis of Rates and Victim Characteristics.* Washington, DC: Government Printing Office.
Hirschi, T.
1969 *Causes of Delinquency,* Berkeley, University of California Press.
Hirschi, T. and M. Gottfredson
1983 "Age and the explanation of crime." *American Journal of Sociology,* 89: 522-584.
Hirschi, T. and M. J. Hindelang
1977 "Intelligence and delinquency: A revisionist view." *American Sociological Review* 42: 571-587.
Hirschi, T. and H. C. Selvin
1973 *Principles of Survey Analysis.* New York: Free Press.

Hirschi, T. and R. Stark
1969 "Hellfire and delinquency." *Social Problems* 17: 202-213.
Hogarth, R. M.
1980 *Judgment and Choice: The Psychology of Decision.* Chichester, UK: Wiley.
Hough, M. and P. Mayhew
1983 *The British Crime Survey: First Report.* London: Her Majesty's Stationery Office.
Hoult, T. F.
1974 *Dictionary of Modern Sociology.* Totowa, NJ: Littlefield, Adams.
Hunter, A.
1978 *Symbols of Incivility: Social Disorder and Fear of Crime in Urban Neighborhoods.* Presented at the annual meeting of the American Society of Criminology, Dallas, TX.
Hyman, H.
1953 "The value systems of different classes," in R. Bendix and S. M. Lipset (eds.) *Class, Status and Power.* New York: Free Press.
Ittelson, W. H., H. M. Prohansky, L. Rivlin, and G. H. Winkel
1974 *An Introduction to Environmental Psychology.* New York: Holt, Rinehart & Winston.
Jacobs, D.
1981 "Inequality and economic crime." *Sociology and Social Research* 66: 12-28
Janowitz, M.
1975 "Sociological theory and social control." *American Journal of Sociology* 81: 82-108.
Janson, C.
1982 *Delinquency Among Metropolitan Boys.* Stockholm, Sweden: University of Stockholm.
Jeffery, C.
1972 "This historical development of criminology," in H. Mannheim (ed.) *Pioneers in Criminology.* Montclair: Patterson Smith.
Jensen, G. F.
1972 "Delinquency and adolescent self conceptions: A study of the personal relevance of infraction." *Social Problems* 20: 84-103.
Jensen, G. F. and D. Rojeck
1979 *Delinquency: A Sociological View.* Lexington: D. C. Heath.
Johnson, R. E.
1979 *Juvenile Delinquency and its Origins.* Cambridge, MA: Cambridge University Press.
Johnstone, J.
1978 "Social class, social areas, and delinquency." *Sociology and Social Research* 63: 49-72.
Kasarda, J. and M. Janowitz
1974 "Community attachment in mass society." *American Sociological Review* 47: 427-433.
Kobrin, S.
1982 "The uses of the life history document for the development of delinquency theory," in the Jack Roller and J. Snodgrass, *The Jack-Roller at Seventy.* Lexington, MA: D. C. Heath.

Kornhauser, R.
1978 *Social Sources of Delinquency*. Chicago: University of Chicago Press.

Krohn, M., R. Akers, M. Radosevich, and L. Lanza-Kaduce
1980 "Social status and deviance." *Criminology* 18: 303-318.

Land, K. C. and M. Felson
1976 "A general framework for building dynamic macro social indicator models: Including an analysis of changes in crime rates and police expenditures." *American Journal of Sociology* 82 (3): 565-604.

Landers, D. M. and D. M. Landers
1978 "Socialization via interscholastic athletics: Its effects on delinquency." *Sociology of Education* 51 (4): 299-303.

Laub, J. H.
1983a *Trends in Juvenile Criminal Behavior in the United States: 1973-1981*. Working paper 24. Albany, NY: Michael J. Hindelang Criminal Justice Research Center.
1983b *Juvenile Criminal Behavior in the United States: An Analysis of Offender and Victim Characteristics*. Working Paper 25. Albany, NY: Michael J. Hindelang Criminal Justice Research Center.
1984 "Talking about crime: Oral history in criminology and criminal justice." *Oral History Review* 12: 29-42.

Lehnen. R. G. and A. J. Reiss
1978 "Response effects in the national crime survey." *Victimology* 3: 110-124.

Lerman, P.
1968 "Individual values, peer values, and subcultural delinquency." *American Sociological Review* 33: 219-235.

Levin, Y. and A. Lindesmith
1937 "English ecology and criminology of the past century." *Journal of Criminal Law and Criminology* 27: 801-816.

Liberson, S., G. Dalto, and M. Johnson
1975 "The courses of mother-tongue diversity in nations." *American Journal of Sociology* 81 (July): 34-61.

Liberson, S. and K. Hansen
1974 "National development, mother-tongue diversity and the comparative study of nations." *American Sociological Review* 39 (August): 523-541.

Lincoln, J. and G. Zeitz
1980 "Organizational properties from aggregate data: Separating individual and structural effects." *American Sociological Review* 45: 391-408.

Liska, A., J. Lawrence, and M. Benson
1981 "Perspectives on the legal order: The capacity for social control." *American Journal of Sociology* 87: 413-426.

Lofland, L.
1973 *A World of Strangers*. New York: Basic Books.

Maccoby, E., J. Johnston, and R. Church
1958 "Community integration and the social control of juvenile delinquency." *Journal of Social Issues* 14: 38-51.

Matza, D.
1964 *Delinquency and Drift*. New York: John Wiley.

McDermott, M. J.

1979 *The Criminal Behavior of Juveniles and Adults: Comparison Within Crime Categories*. Ph.D. dissertation, School of Criminal Justice, State University of New York at Albany.

Mednick, S. A. and J. Volavaka

1980 "Biology and crime," in N. Morris and M. Tonry (eds.) *Crime and Justice* (Vol. 2). Chicago: University of Chicago Press.

Merton, R. K.

1938 "Social structure and anomie." *American Sociological Review* 3: 672.

Messner, S.

1982 "Poverty, inequality and the urban homicide rate." *Criminology* 20: 103-114.

1983a "Regional and racial effects on the urban homicide rate: The subculture of violence revisited." *American Journal of Sociology* 88: 997-1007.

1983b "Regional differences in the economic correlates of the urban homicide rate: Some evidence of the importance of cultural context." *Criminology* 21: 477-488.

Michael, J.

1963 *An Empirical Evaluation of the Culture Conflict Theory as an Explanation of Juvenile Delinquency*. Unpublished paper, Columbia University, New York School of Social Work Research Center.

Miller, D. C.

1977 *Handbook of Research Design and Measurement*. New York: David McKay.

Miller, S. M. and P. Roby

1970 *Future and Inequality*. New York: Basic Books.

Miller, W. B.

1958 "Lower Class culture as a generating milieu of gang delinquency." *Journal of Social Issues* 14: 5-19.

Monahan, J.

1981 *Predicting Violent Behavior: An Assessment of Clinical Techniques*. Newbury Park, CA: Sage.

National Commission of the Causes and Prevention of Violence

1969 *Crimes of Violence* (Vol. 13). Washington, DC: Government Printing Office.

Nerlove, M.

1965 *Estimation and Identification of Cobb-Douglas Production Functions*. Chicago: Rand McNally.

Nettler, G.

1961 "Good men, bad men and the perception of reality." *Sociometry* 24: 279.

1978 *Explaining Crime* (2nd ed.). New York: McGraw-Hill.

Newman, O.

1972 *Defensible Space*. New York: Collier.

Paez, A. L.

1983 *Criminal Victimization in the U.S., 1980-81: Changes Based on New Estimates*. Washington, DC: U.S. Department of Justice, Bureau of Justice Statistics.

Parker, R.

1983 *Poverty, Inequality and Type of Homicide*. Presented at the annual meeting of the American Society of Criminology, Denver, CO.

Parker, R. and M. Smith
1979 "Deterrence, poverty, and type of homicide." *American Journal of Sociology* 85: 614-624.

Parsons, T.
1937 *The Structure of Social Action* (Vol. 1). New York: Free Press.

Penick, B. and M. Owens, III (eds.)
1976 *Surveying Crime.* Final Report of the Panel for the Evaluation of Crime Survey, Committee on National Statistics, National Research Council, National Academy of Sciences, Washington, DC.

Phillipson, M.
1974 *Understanding Crime and Delinquency.* Chicago: Aldine.

Piliavin, I., R. Gartner, G. Thornton, and R. Matsueda
1986 "Crime, deterrence and choice." *American Sociological Review* 51: 101.

Plummer, K.
1983 *Documents of Life.* London: George Allen & Unwin.

Polk, K., D. Frease, and F. Richmond
1974 "Social class, school experience and delinquency." *Criminology* 12: 84-96.

Quinney, R.
1970 *The Social Reality of Crime.* Boston: Little, Brown.
1975 *Criminology.* Boston: Little, Brown.

Quinney, R. and J. Wilderman
1977 *The Problem of Crime: A Critical Introduction to Criminology* (2nd ed.). New York: Harper & Row.

Radzinowicz, L.
1963 *Ideology and Crime.* New York: Columbia University Press.

Rainwater, L.
1970 *Behind Ghetto Walls: Black Families in a Federal Slum.* Chicago: Aldine.

Redl, F. and D. Wineman
1951 *Children Who Hate.* New York: Free Press.

Reiss, A. J.
1976 "Settling the frontiers of a pioneer in American criminology: Henry McKay," pp. 64-88 in J. F. Short, Jr. (ed.) *Delinquency, Crime, and Society.* Chicago: University of Chicago Press.

Reiss, A. J. and A. Rhodes
1961 "The distribution of juvenile delinquency in the social class structure." *American Sociological Review* 26: 720-732.

Robbins, L. N., R. S. Jones, and G. E. Murphy
1966 "School milieu and school problems of negro boys." *Social Problems* 13: 428-436.

Robin, G. P.
1969 "Anti-poverty programs and delinquency." *Journal of Criminal Law, Criminology and Police Science* 60 (Fall): 323-331.

Robinson, W.
1959 "Ecological correlations and the behavior of individuals." *American Sociological Review* 15: 351-357.

Roncek, D.
1981 "Dangerous places: Crime and residential environment." *Social Forces* 60: 74-96.

Rosenfeld, R.
1982 *Inequality, Relative Deprivation and Crime: Explaining Some Discrepant Findings*. Presented at the annual meetings of the American Society of Criminology, Toronto, Canada.
1984 "Urban crime rates: The effects of inequality, welfare dependency, region, and race," in J. Bryne and R. J. Sampson (eds.) *The Social Ecology of Crime: Theory, Research, and Public Policy*. New York: Springer.

Rossi, P., E. Waite, C. Bose, and R. Berk
1974 "The seriousness of crime: Normative structure and individual differences." *American Sociological Review* 39: 224-237.

Sampson, R. J.
1983a *The Neighborhood Context of Criminal Victimization*. Ph.D. dissertation, State University of New York at Albany.
1983b "Structural density and criminal victimization." *Criminology* 21 (May): 276-293.
1985a "Neighborhood and crime: The structural determinants of personal victimization." *Journal of Research in Crime and Delinquency* 22: 7-40.
1985b "Race and criminal violence: A demographically disaggregated analysis of urban homicide." *Crime & Delinquency* 31: 47-82.

Sampson, R. J. and T. C. Castellano
1982 "Economic inequality and personal victimization: An areal perspective." *British Journal of Criminology* 22 (2): 363-385.

Savitz, L.
1970 "Delinquency and migration," in M. Wolfgang, L. Savitz, and N. Johnson (eds.) *Sociology of Crime and Delinquency*. New York: John Wiley.

Schafer, W. E.
1969 "Participation in interscholastic athletics and delinquency: A preliminary study." *Social Problems* 17 (1): 40-47.

Schur, E. M.
1971 *Labeling Deviant Behavior*. New York: Harper & Row.

Sechrest, D. K.
1969 "Comparisons of inmates' and staff's judgments of the severity of offenses." *Journal of Research in Crime and Delinquency* 6: 41-55.

Sellin, T.
1938 *Culture Conflict and Crime*. New York: Social Science Research Council.

Shaw, C. R.
1930 *The Jack Roller: A Delinquent Boy's Own Story*. Chicago: University of Chicago Press (reprinted as Phoenix Edition, 1966).
1938 *Brothers in Crime*. Chicago: University of Chicago Press.

Shaw, C. R. and H. D. McKay
1929 *Delinquent Areas*. Chicago: University of Chicago Press.
1942 *Juvenile Delinquency and Urban Areas*. Chicago: University of Chicago Press.

Shaw, J., Jr. and F. I. Nye
1958 "Extent of unrecorded juvenile delinquency: Tentative conclusions." *Journal of Criminal Law and Criminology* 49: 296-302.

Short, J. F., R. Rivera, and R. Tennyson
1965 "Perceived opportunities, gang membership and delinquency." *American Sociological Review* 30: 56-67.

Short, J. and R. Strodbeck
1965 *Group Process and Gang Delinquency*. Chicago: University of Chicago Press.

Simcha-Fagan, O.
1983 *Delinquency in Environmental Context: A Two Tier Study*. New York: University, School of Public Health.

Simcha-Fagan, O. and R. Sampson
1982 The Urban Areas and Youth Project: A Bilevel Analysis of Adolescent Presented at the Psychiatric Epidemiology Research Seminar, Columbia University, New York.

Simon, R.
1975 *The Contemporary Woman and Crime*. Washington, DC: Government Printing Office.

Singer, S.
1981 "Homogeneous victim-offender populations: A review and some research implications." *Journal of Criminal Law and Criminology* 72 (2): 779-788.

Skogan, W.
1975 "Measurement problems in official and survey crime rates." *Journal of Criminal Justice* 3: 17-32.

Skogan, W. and M. Maxfield
1981 *Coping with Crime: Individual and Neighborhood Reactions*. Newbury Park, CA: Sage.

Skinner, B. F.
1978 *Reflections on Behaviorism and Society*. Englewood Cliffs, NJ: Prentice-Hall.

Smith, S. J.
1982 "Victimization in the inner city." *British Journal of Criminology* 22 (2): 386-402.

Sobel, M.
1981 *Lifestyle and Social Structure: Concept, Definitions, Analysis*. New York: Academic Press.

Solicitor General of Canada
1983 *Victims of Crime* (Bulletin 1). Ottawa, Ontario: Research and Statistics Group.

Sparks, R. F.
1982 *Research on Victims of Crime: Accomplishments, Issues, and New Directions*. Washington, DC: Government Printing Office.

Sparks, R. F., H. G. Genn, and D. J.Dodd
1977 *Surveying Victims: A Study of the Measurement of Criminal Victimization*. New York: John Wiley.

Stark, R., R. Finke, and L. Kent
forth-coming "Going straight is growing up: A longitudinal coming study of delinquency."

Stark, R., L. Kent, and D. Doyle
1981 "Religion and delinquency: The ecology of a 'lost' relationship." *Journal of Research in Crime and Delinquency* 18: 1.

Steinmetz, C.H.D.
1979 *An (Empirically Tested) Analysis of Victimization Risks*. Presented at the Third International Symposium in Victimology, Research and Documentation Centre, Ministry of Justice, The Hague, Netherlands.

Stuart, J.
1936 "Mobility and delinquency." *American Journal of Orthopsychiatry* 6: 286-293.

Sullenger, T. E.
1950 "The social significance of mobility: An Omaha study." *American Journal of Sociology* 55: 559-564.

Sutherland, E. H.
1939 *Principles of Criminology* (3rd ed.). Chicago: J.B. Lippincott.

Suttles, G.
1968 *Social Order of the Slum*. Chicago: University of Chicago Press.

Sveri, K.
1982 "Comparative analyses of crime by means of victim surveys: The Scandinavian experience," pp. 209-219 in H. J. Schneider (ed.) *The Victim in International Perspectives*. Berlin: Walter de Gruyter.

Taylor, I., P. Walton, and J. Young
1973 *The New Criminology*. New York: Harper & Row.

Taylor, R. B., S. Gottfredson, and S. Brower
1984 "Block crime and fear: Defensible space, local social ties and territorial functioning." *Journal of Research in Crime and Delinquency* 21: 4.

Thomas, C. W.
1976 "Public opinion on criminal law and legal sanctions: An examination of two conceptual models." *Journal of Criminal Law and Criminology* 67: 110-116.

Thornberry, T. and M. Farnworth
1982 "Social correlates of criminal involvement." *American Sociological Review* 47: 505-518.

Thrasher, F. M.
1927 *The Gang*. Chicago: University of Chicago Press.

Tilly, C.
1973 "Do communities act?" *Sociological Inquiry* 43: 206-240.

Tittle, C. R., W. J. Villemez, and D. A. Smith
1978 "The myth of social class and criminality: An empirical assessment of the empirical evidence." *American Sociological Review* 43: 643-656.

Toch, H.
1977 *Living in Prison: The Ecology of Survival*. New York: Free Press.
1979 "Perspectives on the offender," in H. Toch (ed.) *Psychology of Crime and Criminal Justice*. New York: Holt, Rinehart & Winston.
1980 *Violent Men*. Cambridge, MA: Schenckman.

U.S. Bureau of the Census
no date *Survey Documentation: National Crime Survey*. Washington, DC: U.S. Department of Commerce.

U.S. Department of Justice, Bureau of Justice Statistics
1982 *Criminal Victimization in the United States, 1980*. National Crime Survey Report, NCJ-84015. Washington, DC: Government Printing Office.

Vold, G. B.
1958 *Theoretical Criminology*. New York: Oxford University Press.

Vold, G. B. and T. S. Bernard
1979 *Theoretical Criminology* (2nd ed.). New York: Oxford University Press.

Voss, H. and D. Peterson
1971 *Ecology, Crime and Delinquency*. New York: Appleton-Century Crofts.

Warren, R.
1978 *Community in America*. Chicago: Rand McNally.
Webster, W. H.
1981 *Crime in the U.S., 1980*. Washington, DC: Government Printing Office.
Wellman, B.
1979 "The community question: The intimate networks of east Yorkers." *American Journal of Sociology* 84: 1201-1231.
Wiatrowski, M. D., D. Greswold, and M. K. Roberts
1981 "Social control theory and delinquency." *American Sociological Review* 46 (5): 525-541.
Williams, K.
1984 "Economic sources of homicide." *American Sociological Review* 49: 283-289.
Wilson, J. Q.
1975 *Thinking about Crime*. New York: Random House.
Wilson, J. Q. and R. Hernnstein
1985 *Crime and Human Nature*. New York: Simon & Schuster.
Wirth, L.
1938 "Urbanism as a way of life." *American Journal of Sociology* 44: 1-24.
Wolfgang, M.
1958 *Patterns of Criminal Homicide*. New York: John Wiley.
Wolfgang, M. and F. Ferracuti
1967 *The Subculture of Violence: Toward an Integrated Theory in Criminology*. London: Travistock.
Wolfgang, M., R. M. Figlio, and T. Sellin
1972 *Delinquency in a Birth Cohort*. Chicago: University of Chicago Press.
Wright, K. N.
1985 "Developing the prison environment inventory." *Journal of Research in Crime and Delinquency* 22: 257-277.
Yiannakis, A.
1976 "Delinquent tendencies and participation in an organized sports program." *Research Quarterly* 47 (4): 845-849.
Young, V.
1979 "Victims of female offenders," in W. H. Parsonage (ed.) *Perspectives on Victimology*. Newbury Park, CA: Sage.
Zimring, F.
1981 "Kids, groups and crime: Some implications of a well known secret." *Journal of Criminal Law and Criminology* 72: 867-885.

About the Authors

Lawrence E. Cohen is Professor of Sociology at Indiana University, Bloomington. His journal publications center on decision making in the juvenile courts and explication of the "routine activity theory" of crime. He is on the editorial board of several social science journals, and was a consulting editor of the *American Sociological Review*. He is pursuing crime forecasting work on a National Science Foundation project with Kenneth Land.

Roger Finke is an Assistant Professor at Loyola University, Chicago. He and Rodney Stark are collaborating on a book about the history of religion in the United States.

James Garofalo is Director of the Hindelang Criminal Justice Research Center at the State University of New York at Albany. With Michael Hindelang and Michael Gottfredson, he authored *Victims of Personal Crime,* and he has written articles concerning victimization, fear of crime, and criminology. Formerly, he was Director of the Research Center for the National Council on Crime and Delinquency.

John S. Goldkamp is Associate Professor of Criminal Justice at Temple University. He is the author of *Two Classes of Accused, Policy Guidelines for Bail* (with Michael Gottfredson), and articles on bail and pretrial detention.

Michael R. Gottfredson is Associate Professor of Management and Policy and of Psychology at the University of Arizona. Formerly, he was Director of the Criminal Justice Research Center in Albany, New York. He has authored articles on victimization, the criminal justice process, and crime policy. His books include *Decisionmaking in Criminal Justice* (with Don Gottfredson) and *Policy Guidelines for Bail* (with John Goldkamp).

Travis Hirschi is Professor of Sociology and of Management and Policy at the University of Arizona. His books include *Delinquency Research* (with Hanan Selvin), *Causes of Delinquency,* and *Measuring Delinquency* (with Michael Hindelang and Joseph Weis). He is Past President of the American Society of Criminology.

Lori Kent is an Assistant Professor at the University of Virginia, where she is engaged in research on the rise of higher education in the United States.

Kenneth C. Land is Professor and Chair, Department of Sociology, Duke University. He is currently examining changes in crime rates and crime distributions in post-World War II United States.

John H. Laub is Associate Professor in the College of Criminal Justice at Northeastern University. He recently completed a research project examining trends and patterns in serious juvenile crime. His book, *Criminology in the Making: An Oral History,* was published by Northeastern University Press.

Robert J. Sampson is Assistant Professor, Department of Sociology, University of Illinois. He is currently analyzing victimization and offender data using measurement models. His interest in neighborhood or community effects on crime is reflected in numerous scholarly publications.

Rodney Stark is Professor of Sociology and Comparative Religion at the University of Washington. He has published eleven books, among which are such recent titles as *The Future of Religion, Sociology,* and *American Piety.*

Hans Toch is Professor of Psychology at the Graduate School of Criminal Justice, State University of New York at Albany. His books include *Violent Men, Agents of Change,* and *Living in Prison.* His book *Men in Crisis* received the Hadley Cantril Award.

Joseph G. Weis is Associate Professor of Sociology and Director of the Center for Law and Justice at the University of Washington. He has directed a series of national-level studies of delinquent behavior and is editor of *Criminology.*

Leslie T. Wilkins is Research Professor of Criminal Justice at the School of Criminal Justice at the State University of New York at Albany. Among his many works are *Social Deviance, Evaluation of Penal Measures,* and *Consumerist Criminology.*

NOTES

NOTES

NOTES